WITH SHERMAN TO THE SEA

A Drummer's Story of the Civil War

April, 1862

Cord is off to the war, aged 13.

WITH SHERMAN TO THE SEA

A *Drummer's Story of the Civil War*

as related by
CORYDON EDWARD FOOTE

to

OLIVE DEANE HORMEL

with a foreword by
ELIZABETH YATES

THE JOHN DAY COMPANY
NEW YORK

© 1960 by Olive Deane Hormel

All rights reserved. This book, or parts thereof, must not be reproduced in any form without permission. Published by The John Day Company, 62 West 45th Street, New York 36, N.Y., and on the same day in Canada by Longmans, Green & Company, Toronto.

Library of Congress Catalogue Card Number: 60-12890

Manufactured in the United States of America

A PATHFINDER BOOK REPRINT EDITION
Printed in the United States of America
ISBN-13: 978-1951682590

In loving memory
of
Katherine Foote Kline
Cord's only daughter
without whom this book
could not have been written

FOREWORD

OLIVE DEANE HORMEL, long a friend of mine in the East, had moved to San Francisco and I had not seen her for some time. Last spring, on a visit to the West Coast, I spent an afternoon with her. When I asked her what she had been doing recently, she pointed to a pile of typed pages on a nearby table and said that she had been going over some reminiscences of a Civil War drummer, which she had written down at the time they were given her.

"You mean you actually knew such a person?"

"Yes, indeed. He was a lifelong, honored resident of Flint, Michigan, which was once my home."

I urged her to tell me more.

"I don't suppose there has been anything in all history quite like the drummer boys of the Civil War," she began. "They were loyal, intrepid lads, most of them only in their teens, but they drummed and marched, foraged and fought through the years of conflict. Designated as 'musicians' on the regimental rosters, they served in many different capacities and always seemed to be at the forefront."

As I listened, Olive told me the fascinating story of Corydon Edward Foote, who had enlisted as a drummer boy when he was one day over thirteen, with the Michigan Tenth Infantry. It was a thrilling story of campaigns, marches, and hard-fought battles; of gallant heroism and grim hardship. Through it all echoed the sound of the drumbeats that began in Flint in 1862 when the regiment was organized and ceased only when the regiment was disbanded some months after the end of the war.

When I asked her how she ever got such a story, she gave me the fully as fascinating account of how she met and talked with Cord Foote. He was near ninety at the time, but the years of warfare had made an indelible impression on him and could be recalled with clarity and vigor.

She was living in Owosso, not far from Flint, and had become acquainted with a Mrs. Katherine Kline who was soon to be known affectionately as Katie. Their conversation was often of books, for Olive's work at the time was connected with lecturing and reviewing, as well as some writing. Katie spoke of her father, Cord Foote, with whom she lived, thinking that Olive would be interested in his story.

Olive's first meeting with him was followed by regular visits. The Foote home, on one of the old residential streets in Flint, was a tall, turreted Victorian house set in an attractive lawn and shaded by great elms. It had a porte-cochere, a drive that encircled the whole, and a stable at the rear. The Footes were one of the last families in Flint to "keep a carriage." Mrs. Foote had died when Katie, their only child, was a little girl. Katie had continued to make her home with her father even after her marriage.

"Cord looked very much like pictures of Mark Twain," Olive explained, "even to the white mustache, though without quite so much hair, and he smoked cigars. He was erect, slender, active. His eyes were very blue and he read without glasses. His hands were small and neat, and he was almost totally deaf. As soon as he knew that I wanted to hear about his years as a drummer boy, he got me in a corner on a hard window seat, sat directly in front of me in his favorite rocking chair, and started to talk at the top of his lungs. I could hardly ask him a question. I could only tell him to stop. When I could listen no more, I held up both my hands. That alone would end the day.

"After that first meeting I went back, week after week, writing down everything he said in my little blue notebook. Katie was usually near, ready to help in bringing from boxes and drawers treasures and mementos of her father's war years. There were any number of pictures of the men he soldiered with and of the officers who commanded them; there was his descriptive roll, and there were letters on yellowed sheets of army paper that he had written home and his mother had saved.

"Cord often had his regimental drum beside him. It was a handsome snare drum with silver instead of leather on the sides for tuning. He loved to play it and would make a terrible din on it at the slightest provocation, adding to his story by beating out marches and calls and the elaborate noise he referred to as the 'daddy-mammy.' His memory was clear and it was teeming. He could recite, even—I'm sure—with something of the throb of their original passion, the words of the speaker who first fired him to enlist.

"Often, when I held up my hands and our meeting was over, Cord would pick up his drum and drum me out of the house and down the walk. I can feel myself stiffen now, as I did then, when the tap-a-tap-tap went faster and faster, finally rolling up into a martial rippety-roar that I thought all of Flint must be able to hear! For a long time afterward the drum seemed to be inside me, carrying me on. I knew then how it was that soldiers marched to it, those long weary miles, and how they went in to battle.

"When I had Cord's route well in mind, I covered it myself, driving over it with a friend. It was a beautiful trip, taken in the late fall. I'll never forget Chattanooga and the view out over the Tennessee Valley at night. We were stranded in Atlanta for a time when heavy rains made the red clay roads impassable, but we finally got through to Savannah. We came home, near Thanksgiving, in the worst blizzard I was ever exposed to as we drove from Louisville to South Bend.

"That battle route filled me with added questions. Most of them could be answered by Cord, but for some—particularly those that had to do with military movements—I turned to the Owosso Public Library, which had inherited several sets of the *Official Records of the Civil War*. They were huge, black-bound tomes, each set running to more than a hundred volumes. One of them was an enormous atlas of the Civil War. Every crossroads was marked on it, and I couldn't have got on without it.

"All the incidents Cord told me could be authenticated and orientated with the official records of his regiment. Important or not as they might seem to me, they had their place in the history of the war. It constantly amazed me to discover that everything Cord said could be verified. What he gave me was a faithful accounting of his days in their deadly drabness and their sudden glory. He had such exultation at the outset, and such disillusionment during the long months of uncertainty and inaction. Then he—and always his drum, of course—became part of a victorious momentum as men like Grant and Sherman began to emerge to direct with firmness and assurance the destinies of the Union Army.

Foreword [11]

"For three years Cord drummed men to march and to fight, to mess and to rest. Long as his life was, and he died in 1944 at the age of ninety-five, those were the real years for him. The things that stirred him most thereafter were the Grand Army of the Republic encampments and the Memorial Day parades when the men who had once fought for the Union could get together again, not so much to exchange recent experiences as to relive past ones. He used to tell me about those encampments, describing the shrilling fifes, the rataplan of the drums, and the brave look of the regimental colors when they were uncased—even though they became faded with the years.

"Home from the war, Cord settled down presently and built a tin shop business which prospered—tin cups, milk pails, eaves troughs, tinware of all sorts. Eventually, it occupied the floors above the town's chief hardware store. When I knew him, he had retired and was always working over the lawn of his home place, which he kept beautifully. He was proud of his collection of stuffed birds and of butterflies, which he kept in glass cases in a sort of study he had made in the stable. Nothing ever mattered to him but the Civil War. There was a time, just before and after his marriage, when he was greatly interested in fancy skating. His wife was his partner, and they entered contests together and wore costumes. But after her early passing he gave himself to the solitariness and independence that had marked him from boyhood. His later deafness, which Katie attributed to the din of battle, only accentuated these tendencies.

"He just went ahead, as he always had, doing what he was interested in doing regardless of anyone else. His drum, his stuffed bird collection, his butterflies, and all his various mementos are now in the Flint Historical Museum."

"Wasn't he thrilled to have you write down his reminiscences?" I asked.

Olive laughed. "He was thrilled to have someone to tell them to, to relive them again for someone who wanted to know everything and was willing to listen to the same story over and over again to get it right, but he didn't have the slightest interest in what I did with them."

"And you wrote them down, you verified them, you went over the ground—this story of Cord's is something that should be published!"

She looked at me, considering my words. "Do you really think so? Nothing would make me happier." Then, after a moment, she said, "But there is so much that would have to be done to it. It's so long and discursive, and somehow I can't work on it now. I'm too far away from it all."

I went over to the pile on the table—typed pages, maps, photostats of letters, daguerreotypes of Cord when he went to war. I read a paragraph here and a page there. It was odd, but in that high and lovely room in Olive's San Francisco apartment with the April air fresh from the Bay sweeping through the windows, I could almost hear the distant beat of a drum long silent, a drum that had rallied men at a time when great issues were at stake.

"Olive, would you let me take this back East with me, read it carefully, put it in the hands of a publisher?"

She thought for a moment, then nodded slowly. "What about the work that may need to be done on it? Would you do it?"

I said I would, if it needed anything.

Reading the typed pages led me to see whether there had ever been any other such stories. I found the famous little pamphlet *Drummer Boy of Shiloh* by Vic Reinhardt, published by Terrell in Texas in 1910. I found, too, a book published in 1883 by Houghton Mifflin, *The Recollections of a Drummer-Boy* by Harry M. Kieffer. I found no other memoir. But I learned many interesting things. In the army, from Revolutionary days through the Civil War, drums and

Foreword

fifes were used as signals and for military music. Each company of infantry and artillery had a fifer and a drummer, while the cavalry used buglers. During the Civil War, the youngest wearers of the blue were the drummer boys and the cavalry buglers; and many of them were very young. When Benjamin A. Gould, a Sanitary Commission actuary, compiled vital statistics for 1,012,273 Union volunteers, he listed some ten thousand as being under eighteen when they enlisted:

127 were 13
330 were 14
773 were 15
2758 were 16
6425 were 17

He stated, however, that no true number could ever be arrived at from the muster roles because many boys in their eagerness to go to war misrepresented their ages. The youngest ones, like regimental mascots, received extra attentions and were highly thought of. They showed great stamina, were remarkably resilient, and their buoyancy had a cheerful effect on the older men that resulted in more kindliness amid the ruggedness of camp life; but the boys grew up rapidly under the constant strain and their responsibilities.

The story of Cord's life during the Civil War moved me as it had Olive when she first wrote it down, and it was a joy to work on it, as I did for some weeks. My contribution was minor. For what Olive Hormel had caught, true and vivid, as she listened notebook in hand to Corydon Edward Foote was a piece of our American past. It is all here and it has, I believe, a place in our American present.

ELIZABETH YATES

Peterborough,
New Hampshire.

April, 1960

WITH SHERMAN TO THE SEA

A Drummer's Story of the Civil War

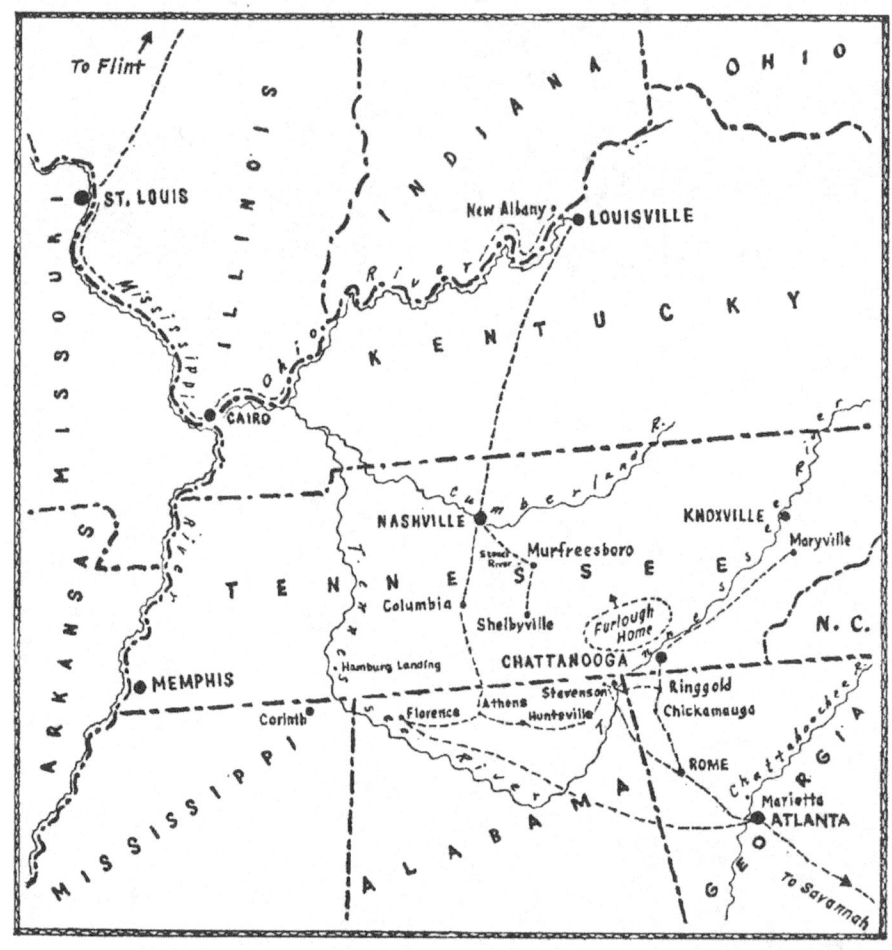

CAMPAIGNING WITH THE MICHIGAN 10TH INFANTRY
1862–1865
I

(A second map appears on page 125)

CHAPTER I

DURING THE EARLY MONTHS of 1861 the northern tide of patriotism was running as high in Flint, Michigan, as it was in Boston, Massachusetts, or in Lawrence, Kansas. Every city and crossroads community, as well as every citizen, from small boys who hoped to grow up quick enough to be soldiers to old men who had fought with Andrew Jackson in the Indian Wars, was inflamed at the secession of the southern states. There was only one word for it—"treason"; and only one name for those perpetrating it—"traitors."

In February, when word reached Flint of the organizing of the Southern Confederacy, a meeting of protest was called. The whole town turned out for the speeches that went on for half the night, interspersed by patriotic music from the local band. A boy, thin and wiry with a shock of thick brown hair and blue eyes that were staring-big, wove in and out among the people until he worked up close to the band; then he squeezed himself into a place beside the drum major, old Pop Lacey who was a veteran of the Indian Wars.

The speaker of the evening ended his address as he quoted words of the recently retired governor, Moses Wisner: " 'We believe that the founders of our government designed it to be perpetual, and we cannot consent to have one star obliterated from our flag. For upwards of thirty years this question of the right of a state to secede has been agitated. It is time it was settled. We ought not to leave it to our children to look after.' "

The drum major led the cheering and the sound of it was louder than anything that had come from his drum.

Then the mayor paid tribute to the newly inaugurated Governor Blair for refusing, with four other northern governors, to send delegates to the "peace-congress at Washington, called by that weakly wavering state of Virginia for purposes of parley and ignoble compromise with the traitor South. Our honorable executive is right," he shouted, as he shifted from scorn to exaltation, then quoted from the recent inaugural, " 'the Federal Government has power to defend itself, and I do not doubt that power will be used to the utmost. It is a question of war that the seceding states have to look in the face!' "

The mayor had expressed in words what every man in the crowd was feeling, and cheering broke out again, wild tumultuous cheering.

The meeting was over and people had turned to go home when a man rushed to the platform from a side entrance. In his hand he held a crumpled copy of the *Detroit Free Press* which had just been brought in by a traveler. Waving it for silence, he read in ringing tones a statement by Senator Chandler, " 'The people of Michigan are opposed to all compromises. They do not believe that any compromise is necessary. They are prepared to stand by the Constitution of the

United States as it is, to stand by the government as it is; aye, sir, to stand by it to blood, if necessary!' "

In a frenzy of cheering, the meeting came to its second end. No one knew exactly what was to be done, or what could be done; but every one present knew that he stood by the Union, whatever that might mean.

The boy, who had been standing close to the band, waited until the drum major picked up his drum and tucked his sticks away, then he trotted along beside him, listening to what he was saying. Pop Lacey wasn't talking to anyone in particular, but he was telling anyone who would listen just what Andy Jackson would have done with those Southern traitors.

Cord Foote nodded, sure that whatever Pop Lacey said was right.

When Fort Sumter was fired on in April it meant war. The national fervor that had been running at full tide reached its flood, and people were swept along in it. From the Atlantic Ocean, north of the Mason-Dixon Line, beyond the mountains and across the Mississippi River, the drumbeat could be heard; it rolled over the plains where farmers were planting corn their wives would harvest, and it echoed within patriot hearts.

President Lincoln issued a call for 75,000 volunteers.

The night in Flint when it was to be read, Cord Foote wove through the crowd to be as near as he could to the Court House steps. Colonel Fenton, who was to read the President's call, was a leading lawyer in town and his military record was well known. The boy with the shock of brown hair and the staring-big eyes gazed up at Colonel Fenton with awe and admiration as he mounted the steps, while a rapt crowd of men and women pressed close. The façade of the wooden Court House was lit by the hot orange light of a hundred torches that flared in the April wind. In the silence that preceded Colonel Fenton, there was nothing to be heard but the hissing of the torches.

Then the colonel's full-toned voice resounded over the crowd and down the tree-lined streets around the Court House into which they had overflowed. As he read the call for volunteers, the cheers of the crowd punctuated its phrases. Cord, standing close and looking up into the speaker's bearded face, quivered with excitement.

"The time for gentle dalliance has long since passed away," Colonel Fenton cried out. "Now, my fellow citizens, the time has come when we must 'strike for our altars and our fires, strike for the green graves of our sires, for God and our native land'!"

Men cheered and shouted. Possessed by patriotism, they were ready to give their lives for the preservation of the Union.

Cord would have given anything he owned—his slingshot or even his collection of stuffed birds—to be the first man up to answer the call for volunteers. Wishing he were a few years older, or a few inches taller, he stood there and watched men surge toward the Court House steps in their eagerness to enlist. He saw his brother George go up, then Charlie Gardner's father, and one after another of the Flint men. He was proud of his brother, but he was envious too.

"Hi there, Cordie, bet you wish you could join up!" one of the men called down to him.

Cord, who looked eleven but felt sixteen, set his lips tight. He knew what he wanted to do—join the Michigan First Infantry and go off to fight the Rebels. There might be a chance of a place that someone as small as he could fill, he told himself, as he turned away from the Court House, determined to keep a sharp watch.

The days that followed were gala days, no more so for Flint than for Chicago or for any northern city. Flags flew from stores and houses, bands played at all hours of the day as they marched up and down the main street or stood before the Court House. A fife and drum corps paraded the streets nearly every night with a torchlight procession falling in behind whenever there were to be speeches. The lilt of bugles and the rattle of drums seemed as much a part of each day as April's alternate sunshine and showers. Then the men in their newly issued uniforms, carrying their untried guns, commenced to leave. Charlie Gardner's father's company was the first to go—the "Flint Union Grays" they called themselves—ordered into rendezvous at Detroit with the Michigan Second. Two companies remained to drill daily in the public square, charge picket fences along highways, and maneuver across country, and Cord Foote and Charlie Gardner were their tireless spectators.

In late May the town paper, *The Wolverine Citizen*, carried an exultant story of the arrival of the Michigan First Infantry in Washington a full week earlier than the President's call required, the first regiment to report from the West. They had paraded to the White House and were praised by President Lincoln for their promptness and soldierly appearance. Flint was agog at this distinction, and that night Cord and a bevy of small boys helped pile boards and boxes in a huge pyramid topped by an empty tar barrel for a flaming display of patriotism that surpassed anything the old Court House had ever looked upon.

Then came the news of the defeat at Bull Run. The shock was somewhat softened for the people of Flint by the fact that the Michigan Second and Third were cited as regiments that had helped stem the rout. Charlie Gardner promptly became a hero through his father's participation. Charlie had been learning to play the drum and he soon became a hero in his own right when Captain Guild, who had been their schoolteacher, was persuaded to take him as drummer for the "Fenton Light Guard." That was Cord's brother George's company, named in honor of Colonel Fenton who now became its commander when, in August, they went to Grand Rapids to rendezvous with the Michigan Eighth. It was hard for Cord to believe that the smartly stepping uniformed drummer who led off amid applause and tears was his old friend Charlie Gardner.

Life was an ache of emptiness in the weeks that followed as Cord went about his chores, then fed his bantams and cared for the heifer. It might have been unbearable but for the assurance that Flint would soon be rendezvous for a new regiment to be organized as the Michigan Tenth. In November the field officers came from Detroit, resplendent in brass buttons and Federal blue. Their rough camp was constructed less than two blocks from the Foote homestead. Cord lived in its throb and stir as mobilization began and drums and bugles once more signaled the events of the day.

Organization of the regiment was nearly completed when it became known that Company F lacked a drummer. Cord saw the chance for which he had been waiting. Approaching Pop Lacey, who was in charge of the Drum Corps, he saluted smartly. It was a carefully planned salute that he had been practicing for a long time.

"I'd like to be drummer for Company F, sir," he said, with as matter-of-fact an air as he could muster.

"Well, if it isn't Little Foote!" exclaimed the drum major with pleased surprise, while Cord held desperately to his carefully cultivated military bearing. "I didn't know you could drum, son. By the Lord, you look as if it would do you out to carry a drum! But, if you can handle the sticks as smartly as you salute, we might try to take you on. S'pose you do a turn or two for me on that drum over there."

"Please, sir, I don't know how to drum," Cord said, "but I can learn. I know I can learn, because I've been watching you ever since I was a little tyke. And I used to watch Charlie Gardner, too. I know I can get the hang of it with a little showing."

"Charlie Gardner was a lot bigger than you."

"Yes, sir."

There was a pause while the drum major studied him and Cord, standing stiffly at attention, knew that his longed-for enlistment was at stake.

"What's your name, Little Foote?"

"Cord, sir. Coridon * Edward Foote."

"Well, Cord," the major said with the hint of a smile, "we haven't any time to lose. Bring me that loose board over there, and let's get at it."

Pop Lacey produced two of the several pairs of drumsticks he always had about his person and offered one of the pairs to Cord. He sat down and spread the board between himself and Cord, and lessons began.

"It's all in the way you hold your sticks, firm but not rigid," the drum major said, the ease of long-time proficiency in his words. "The upper, or left hand, is the more difficult, so begin with that."

Cord shifted the sticks to get them right.

"Take the stick firmly between your thumb and two middle fingers and let it rest on the third finger, a little above the middle joint." He moved his hand over Cord's to aid the boy's finger position. "There, you have it!"

For all his eagerness to succeed, Cord felt that his fingers might have been toes so awkward was he with them; but Pop Lacey was understanding.

"You'll have to give that left hand exercise to bring it up to the right. Tie your shoes with it, button your shirt, make it do the things your other hand does easily. The right hand

---

* The spelling that he used in his letters. In later life, he adopted the spelling Corydon.

is lower in position and you hold that stick fast with the little finger. That's the way! Now, see if you can close a roll."

"Please, sir?"

"Two strokes down with the upper hand, two with the lower. Repeat and quicken the time. Repeat. Repeat."

Cord did the best he could, then he looked up despairingly.

"You're trying to go too fast, Cordie, and you can't go fast till you've mastered your hands. It's easy enough to make a noise on a drum, but to pick the beats off at different timings and with different strengths is the trick. You'll make a drummer if you keep at it."

Cord looked hopeful but bewildered.

"Here's a pair of hickory sticks," the drum major said. "Practice wherever you can find a flat surface, and come back tomorrow for another lesson."

Cord practiced at home whenever he had a spare moment, and every day he presented himself before Pop Lacey for a lesson. His hands began to obey him. Instead of fumbling hesitant sounds he could produce sharp clean taps, but slowly. His lack of speed worried him.

"It will come in time. Take it slow while you're learning and you'll develop no bad habits," Pop Lacey said comfortingly. "And remember, elbows out. The real force comes from your shoulders not your hands."

"Yes, sir."

"I've told Captain Beach about you, Cordie, and he says you're to join the other drummers of the regiment at their practice sessions."

Cord's eyes shone. "You mean I'm to sit with George Jay and Ira Miles?"

"And all the rest. There are eighteen of us in the Drum Corps, if I count myself."

Now, twice daily, Cord joined the Drum Corps as they sat

in a row with a long board in front of them and tapped out turns to the drum major's directions. Mastering the single alternate strokes, then the double, they advanced to the more difficult paradiddles and flamdiddles, then the rolls—those rapid beats in quick succession which were used to convey military commands.

"Let her go now, boys," the drum major said.

The drummers, tapping twice for each hand movement, increased their speed until they reached a roll.

Pop Lacey smiled broadly as the roll continued and gained in volume, then he raised his hands for the drummers to stop. "That's the best daddy-mammy I've ever heard played on a board. You're ready for drums now."

Cord had been wondering how he could gain his parents' permission, without which enlistment would be impossible. On the day of his graduation from a practice board to the promise of a snare drum, it happened that his mother was away from home. Cord had been told to present himself for a parade that night. Wearing a borrowed drum, he stepped along in the front rank of the Drum Corps, playing as smartly as the older drummers. His father, watching the parade, was proud of his son, and not altogether surprised to see where he was and what he was doing. He had guessed what Cord was up to when he had heard the muffled sounds coming during the past weeks sometimes from the house, sometimes from the barn. Cord felt that once his father saw him drumming he would not have to work too hard to get his permission for enlistment. His mother he would approach when she returned from taking care of his sick brother, Will.

The next morning Cord went to his father's harness shop and pushed open the door. The bell tinkled as the door closed behind him, and Cord's father came out from the workroom to see what he could do for a customer. Cord looked small but determined as he asked his father to help him enlist.

Together they went to the headquarters of the Michigan Tenth.

"I'm proud of the boy's spunk, Colonel Lum," Cord heard his father say. "Get him through if you can. He's that set on it he'll go anyway, I guess, but his mother and I will feel better to have it as regular as possible."

Colonel Lum turned to Cord. "How old are you?" he asked.

"Twelve, sir."

Colonel Lum promised to do what he could. Cord was sworn into state service and given his own drum.

From then on he drilled daily with the regiment and continued his own practice sessions, generally in the barn with the chickens, cows and family horse as audience. School was forgotten. It had occupied little place in his mind ever since that night, more than eight months ago, when listening to Colonel Fenton's impassioned words he had been fired with a desire to enlist in the army that was going to save the Union.

It was on January 10, 1862, the day after Cord's thirteenth birthday, that the officer came to muster the volunteers into the United States Army. Colonel Lum told Cord to keep in the background, and that was never difficult for one so small. Cord never knew quite what happened, because he was never officially sworn in, but he was mustered in "sight unseen" with all the late joiners of the regiment, men whose papers were submitted to Washington without ceremony. What Cord knew, when he walked back to his home with a drum on his back and a Federal blue coat two sizes too big for him, was that he was actually enlisted in the United States Army for a period of three years.

Cord's mother could do little but accept the situation. In her heart she was proud of her son, proud of what he wanted to do for his country. She gave her consent, though it had already been assumed, when Cord gave her his solemn promise never to gamble. There was, however, one order which she felt she could give to her small soldier and that was to have his picture taken in uniform and with his drum before he went to war.

Cord acted on it and went to the photographer. He stood at attention while the photographer went through his rigmarole, "Roses are red, violets are blue, and the camera is looking right at YOU." When the daguerreotypes were finished and could be given to his mother, Cord was delighted that the drum had come out so well.

Early in April, the Michigan Tenth received its orders. Flint citizens had presented Colonel Lum with a handsome Stars and Stripes. On a silver band on the staff was inscribed the state motto TUEBOR (I will defend) and the words TENTH REGIMENT, MICHIGAN VOLUNTEER INFANTRY. Uniformed, equipped, and drilled to all but actual fighting, the regiment was ready to march through war to victory under the waving silk of their battle flag.

The day before they left, Cord had a long good-by with his bantams and the heifer. He stood beside the litter of baby rabbits in a box in the barn and wondered how big they would be when he saw them again. Returning to the house, he packed away his collection of birds' eggs and the stuffed birds that he had bagged with his slingshot and mounted himself; then he gave special instructions to his mother as to what she should do with any additions that he might send her. With regimental drum on his back and slingshot in his pocket, he was ready to leave.

Wet and snowy though the morning of the regiment's departure was, people lined the streets to cheer the eleven hundred men of the Tenth Michigan Infantry on their way to war. No one doubted but that they would soon be cheering them home again. Everyone knew that as soon as the Federal forces really got into action, the Rebels would be routed. One by one the lumbering transport wagons filled with grinning, shouting, waving men turned the corner by the Court House and went slowly down the street between lines of wildly shouting people. Flags sagged in the April snow, but nothing could dampen the spirits of those who were going off to war or those who were sending them.

The Drum Corps rode hilariously in the first wagon, shouting gaily to the crowds along the way. It was a slow journey to the neighboring town of Holly, where the regiment was to entrain for Detroit. The horses strained on, the cheers of the crowd died away in the distance, and when the men had no one to shout to they began to sing some of their campground favorites. At every important crossroads, in spite of the raw wet weather, people had gathered, some with flowers to toss into the soldiers' hands, others with food to give them for their journey.

As they approached the tiny town of Whigville, Cord saw his married sister, Hannah, with a group of shawled and aproned women watching their approach from the sheltered porch of a country store. As the Michigan Tenth passed, Hannah waved her apron and called out something cheery, not realizing that her own small brother was among the soldiers. Cord was torn between relief and disappointment that she did not see him, then obeying a sudden impulse, he leaned far over the side of the wagon and shouted to her before it was too late.

"Good-by, Hannah! Good-by! I'm going to war, too!"

Her waving apron dropped. With a shriek of recognition she started toward him. "Cordie, Cordie Foote! Cordie, come back!" she called frantically. "You're too little to go!"

Her cries followed faintly after him as the wagon procession lumbered on, axle-deep in the Michigan mud. Cord saw the women draw her back to the shelter of the porch again.

The boys in the wagon behind the Drum Corps shouted, "Can't stop Little Foote now!"

Cord's heart was high within him. He was doing what he had wanted to do ever since he had heard Colonel Fenton read President Lincoln's call for volunteers. He was going off to war.

CHAPTER II

THE FLAG-DECKED TOWN of Holly gave the Michigan Tenth a tremendous welcome with a band and speeches, then the soldiers were conducted through festive streets to the Detroit and Milwaukee Railway Station where trains with steam up awaited them. In an open space beside the tracks long tables were laid for the regiment's full eleven hundred, and here, in spite of the spitting snow and prevailing wetness, the ladies of the town served a generous dinner. There were hot coffee and beef stew, chicken and biscuits, potatoes and gravy, pork and beans, apple pies by the hundred, gingerbread and jam tarts, doughnuts, chocolate cake. Motherly women and romantic young girls saw to it that every man had his share, especially Little Foote.

Many of the men had never been beyond the borders of their native state; Cord had not been outside his native county. Everything was new and exciting. Going off to war seemed like a kind of glorified Sunday school picnic. As the men poured onto the train, the crowd cheered.

"Hurrah for the Michigan Tenth!"

"Don't let the Rebs shoot you in the back!"

Cord, who still looked eleven but felt more than sixteen, and George Jay, who actually was a lanky sixteen, stood together as the train began to pull away from the station, then they shared a seat.

The snorting, cinder-blowing locomotive with its jolting train of cars was a creature of winged wonder to them both, and their wide-eyed satisfaction in the experience was subject for much good-natured banter in the course of the five hours' ride to Detroit.

"Gosh ding, Cord, we must be goin' fifteen miles an hour!" George said.

"Like to be an engineer when you get big, Little Foote?" one of the men asked.

"Hell, there wouldn't be a live cow left in the country if that young devil ever got loose with a steam engine!" another exclaimed.

"Hang on, boys, we're goin' around a curve!"

Detroit had begun to be used to soldiers but nevertheless the streets were lined with cheering spectators along the course of the short march from the old Milwaukee Station to the Michigan Central.

"Look at the knee-high drummer!"

"Hey, sonny, does your mother know you're out?"

"Tell old Abe there's lots more where you come from!"

Cord stepped along in his smartest form, solemnly erect, eyes rigidly front, using his sticks with the precision he had learned from Old Lacey and outwardly ignoring the crowd. Despite his too-large uniform, he was beginning to enjoy the distinction which his youth and small stature conferred upon him. Folks were not just laughing at him, he told himself. They liked him.

Once on board at Detroit, the two nights and two days

of weary riding that followed might have seemed unbearably long and uncomfortable had it not been for the news of the battle of Shiloh. For months the tide of success had been running almost entirely to the Confederates, and Shiloh was another surge on that tide. It had taken place just three weeks before and reports of it were still coming through. Old Lacey had got hold of a copy of the *Detroit Free Press* and as the train jolted across Indiana and Illinois, southward bound, he read about the battle to members of the Drum Corps. Shiloh seemed as unreal and faraway as all the battles had during the past year except for one thing—a drummer boy had helped turn the tide by sounding the countercharge and leading off at a critical moment.

Pop read how one side had pressed the other until finally the Union soldiers had begun to move forward under a rattling fire of small arms and the steady booming of cannon. The Rebels then had wavered. Cord, as he listened, wished that the eyewitness account had not had quite so much to say about the clouds of rolling smoke, the smell of burning powder, and the din of the battlefield; he wanted to know what happened. Pop paused for a moment to be sure that he had the attention of his listeners, then he read how out of all the confusion a fife had shrilled, drumbeats had sounded, and the Rebel yell had rung out. Under their own artillery fire, the gray line had begun to move forward, bristling with the steel of their bayonets.

"It was the drum that did it," Old Lacey said, admiring valor wherever it might appear. Under that wildly yelling, hard-hitting Rebel charge, the blue line began to break and fall back in disorder across the field.

Pop Lacey folded the paper and put it carefully in his pocket, shaking his head slowly.

Grim and stirring as the account of Shiloh had been, it did not seem real to Cord. It was like a story in a book read by a man who had seen military action long before Cord had been born. But one thing was real: the role of the drummer boy as he transformed faltering men into a fighting force.

"Something's there for each one of us," Old Lacey said as he looked at his boys, confident that each one could do what the unknown drummer boy at Shiloh had done.

Among the drummers of the Tenth, the two who meant most to Cord were George Jay of Company K, and Ira Miles who was second in command to Pop Lacey. Both were adept with their hickory sticks, and Cord gained in skill as he watched them do flams and ruffs, paradiddles and ratamacues, then practiced them on his own drum. DeGraff, who played the bass drum, was someone for whom Cord had great respect; and Hans Schumacher, the bulky German bugler, was the one member of the corps who managed to do things now and then that gave them all a good laugh.

Even on the train the day began with reveille played by bugler and drummers. It closed with tattoo. In between there were calls to mess, and plenty of time for the drummer boys to practice marches and battle calls on a wooden board. The drummers knew the importance of their work, knew that there would be times when the regiment would advance under commands not from its officers but from the drums. It was the drums that would say "Forward," or "Double quick," or "Trail arms" when the words might give not only position but intent away to the enemy. In the thick of battle, it was the drums that would roll out the command "Charge bayonets!" The boys were more aware than ever after the story of the battle of Shiloh that they would not only establish military direction but fire the hearts of the soldiers to carry it out. They practiced willingly, not only with their drum major but by themselves, as the train journeyed on monotonously and they drew near the area of actual fighting, near the time of their own responsibility.

By the end of the second day, it began to seem to the men of the Tenth that they had never been anywhere but in the cramped, ill-smelling inside of a railway train that backed and lurched and stood still quite as much as it went forward. They ached with inactivity and sleeplessness, and the sheer discomfort of close-packed quarters. Some were patient, more were profane, and all rejoiced as they stumbled from their stuffy coaches at the small railway terminus of Illinoistown. From there, the journey south was to be continued by river steamer.

The *Gladiator* awaited them within view on the nearby river, its twin chimneys belching black clouds of smoke, its lights gleaming wanly through the rain-soaked dusk, in what seemed to be a vast gray wilderness of water. There had been heavy rains, and the Mississippi was at flood. As they marched toward it, Cord began to be filled with the dreary wind-swept sound of the too-full river—a ceaseless undertone of mighty murmuring which, as their boat shuddered away from the shaky wharf, seemed to be sweeping them with it into engulfing darkness.

Cord lay for hours that night on the bare wet boards of the open deck which was their only bed, fighting sleep in a kind of instinctive resistance to that ceaseless sound of many waters all around him. It was less sinister in the gray fog of early morning. He awoke stiff with cold and from the unaccustomed hardness of his bed, but he was not so wet and cold as the men about him, for during the night someone had spread an extra coat over him.

That day they reached Cairo. There the *Gladiator* turned up the Ohio River, a waste only a little less wide than the Mississippi. The Ohio, too, had its forlorn fringe of flooded woods and abandoned houses. It was a good day, for they had begun to be used to the sound of the river, and the freedom of the boat after the cramped quarters on the train was a pleasant thing. Cord and George Jay explored the boat from the damp black hold which Cord thought smelled like the cellar at home, to the pilothouse on the upper deck where they watched the husky river pilot, their attention held by the sure skill with which he steered their clumsy boat past shoals and snags and sand bars as it approached the confluence of the Tennessee and Cumberland rivers, then turned it safely into the flooded channel of the Tennessee.

The tall trees which stood on either side, waist-high in the slow-swirling flood, were scarred with recent conflict. Now and again the tangled debris of battle floated past the *Gladiator*, dislodged by the high water. Cord and George Jay stared when they saw the dead body of a horse, mutilated by a bursting shell and swollen. Cord gripped the rail of the boat as a dead soldier, face down and arms spread-eagled, floated by. This was the sodden aftermath of the battles of Shiloh and Pittsburg Landing. This was what war did to living things, what it left behind. Suddenly war became something horribly, sickeningly real. No longer was it only in newspaper accounts or stories on the lips of old men. Cord shut his eyes, but he could not shut away the sights he had seen with them. He wondered numbly if he could keep from running away from a mess like that on the river. He wanted to know how George Jay felt about it. But George, too, was silent.

On the Tennessee it was slower going. They were moving against the current as on the Ohio, but it was in a less clearly marked channel. Now, as they approached enemy territory, every man was ordered below except for a few picked as sharpshooters who were to keep guard on the upper deck. The tangled forests along the Tennessee River were known to be swarming with guerrillas, outlaw marauders who preyed upon both sides.

Cord and George huddled together below deck, close to the level of the moaning river against which the *Gladiator* moved laboriously. To them then, the direst of carnage seemed imminent, and almost any kind of man monster that might appear would have been as credible as a gorilla. But the battle cries their ears were tuned for never came. Instead there was lusty cheering when they presently passed Fort Henry with the Stars and Stripes floating over it. Here, two months before, the Stars and Bars of the Confederacy had been flying, but they had been hauled down when General Grant issued his order of "unconditional surrender" from nearby Fort Donelson on the Cumberland.

"You boys don't know but you'll be drumming for General Grant one of these days," Old Lacey said cheerfully as the *Gladiator* moved on past Fort Henry and they talked of Grant's stirring challenge.

The next day they reached Pittsburg Landing, then were ordered upstream to Hamburg Landing. There the gangplank was dropped and the men of the Michigan Tenth disembarked on a shaky wharf two inches under water. In pouring rain and the waning light of a gray afternoon, they set about making camp in a ragged clearing in the midst of a close-growing forest. Wind sighed through the trees, the river moaned, and the rain seemed to be doing its best to slash through the canvas of their new Sibley tents. It was impossible to get a fire to burn. Supper rations consisted of damp crackers and cold water. But they had reached the battle area at last, after a week's traveling. Now, when the Michigan Tenth received orders, it would be as a unit of the Second Brigade, General Pope's Division, right wing, Army of the Mississippi.

"To your drums," Old Lacey called.

The drummers lined up and sounded tattoo.

After the soldiers had gone to their tents, the members of the Drum Corps went to theirs, rolled up in their blankets and prepared to sleep on the sodden ground.

"If they knew what a nice state we got up in Michigan, they'd fight their plaguy war up there," George Jay said disconsolately.

"Lord only knows who picked out this swamp," grumbled Old Lacey, "but you'd better not be thinking about Michigan."

Cord tried to follow his advice.

They might be in the battle area, but they were not to be immediately engaged in fighting. Reconnaissance and skirmishing were the task of the Tenth for the next few days. When the sun shone, the weather turned steamy hot. The country was vast and wild, rank with thick green undergrowth, and viscid with red mud that bound their every movement. The enemy had retired toward Corinth after the battle of Shiloh, and Corinth was only ten miles crowflight from Hamburg Landing. But ten miles seemed an impenetrable distance in that wet green wilderness flowing with swollen rivers.

"They may call them creeks in these parts," one of the soldiers said as he stood by the swirling water, "but I'd like to see man or beast cross them without a bridge."

By the 8th of May the waters had somewhat subsided. The Second Brigade, to which the Tenth now belonged, was ordered to make a reconnaissance toward Corinth. They were to march light, which meant that their knapsacks and bedrolls were deposited in the Company wagons which would follow while they worked on ahead without encumbrance. It was hard going, but they made six circuitous miles before sunset on a narrow road scarcely more than a trail through the swampy forest. It was tense going, too, with momentary expectation of encounter with the hidden enemy. But the enemy did not appear.

Twilight found the men hot, mud-stained, weary, and faced with the information that the wagon train bearing all their equipment and supplies was stuck in the mud a few miles back. Two crackers, a slice of bacon, and a swallow of coffee—emergency rations from their haversacks—was their meager board that night. Branches broken from the young trees all about them served those ambitious enough to gather them for beds. Cord's bed of beech branches was far from comfortable, but at least it kept him off the ground. He had seen too many squirming, slimy creatures in the boggy country they had marched through not to be glad for even a small elevation.

After reveille the next morning the boys had no duties to perform, so Cord and George Jay set off early to try to find the stalled wagons. In the gray dawn they picked their way among the disgruntled soldiers and went off through the woods to a spring they had seen the day before. There they washed themselves and, after drinking deeply of the fresh cool water, set out on their search. The wagons were not to be found, but as the boys approached a wide clearing they saw a Union regiment drawn up in battle array. The sun had just risen. In its light, blue uniforms and shining arms gleamed brilliantly against the shadowy green of the forest background.

A bugle call, familiar to the boys as one often sounded by their own regimental bugler, shrilled through the silence. It was followed by others less well known, and each one was responded to in turn by a quick change in skirmish formation, deftly performed. It was the most impressive exhibition of mass military dexterity that Cord and George had yet seen. Drawing nearer, they made out the regiment to be the Sixtieth Illinois with which they were to be brigaded.

"Some of those boys can't be much older 'n me," George said respectfully.

The rifles they carried seemed big for them, and in many cases their sword bayonets dragged on the ground.

"Nor me," Cord added.

"Guess we'll all have a chance to grow up together."

The boys watched the Sixtieth Illinois with mounting admiration. When they returned to their own Tenth, still grumbling about the stalled wagons, they told Hans Schumacher of the military spectacle they had just seen.

"Wish we could look like them and drill the way they do," George said. Both he and Cord were more than ever conscious of their mud-stained uniforms and the Tenth's dejected appearance.

"*Ach, Gott!*" the bugler said, as he bit off a large chunk of tobacco in lieu of other breakfast. "You boys ought to know by now dis war ain't no dress parade."

They were quite of a mind with him until the time the wagons came up with them that day, bringing rations.

Next morning, on another prowl after a comfortable night with proper camp equipment and a savory breakfast in the open, Cord and George were again susceptible to the glamour of military parade. This time it was the spectacle of twelve hundred cavalry moving out on a "reconnaissance in force." With swords gleaming, flags streaming in the fresh morning wind, and bugles sounding the advance, they went loping in rhythmic hundreds up over the ragged low hillside to vanish beyond the horizon as if the racing cloud billows had conjured them away. For a time there was a phantom rhythm of hoofbeats in gradual diminuendo. Then all was still.

"It takes the cavalry boys to look like a picture book, don't it, Cord?"

"Yes, but—" Cord paused, "when they get their horses shot

out from under them—" He stopped. All he could see was the bloated body of a horse floating down the Ohio River. Where was his rider now? Cord wondered.

For the next two weeks the Michigan Tenth was occupied in performing a gradual flanking movement upon the enemy stronghold at Corinth. To the Drum Corps it seemed only a weary and senseless process of moving forward three days and falling back one to let other regiments pass whom they later passed again. There was never a glimpse of the enemy, though his skirmish fire and sometimes his cannon could be heard, and it was always near enough to keep them alert. Then, suddenly, on the 26th of May, just a month after their arrival at the front, came the regimental baptism of fire.

As pickets, men of the Tenth were the first to find themselves within bullet range that morning, though they were hidden from the enemy whom they could not see. For two hours they moved along through the swampy forest, under strict orders to refrain from shooting until the enemy came in sight. They felt more like hunted animals than fighting men as they crept through the dense growth and waded through the clinging mud. At noon an orderly brought word that two Rebel brigades were passing along the front of their line to the left.

Lieutenant Colonel Dickerson and Adjutant Cowles hurried forward at once to a point in the woods from which it was thought the Rebel brigades could be seen. A battery of Illinois artillery who called themselves the "Yates Sharpshooters" was rushed into position.

Cord and George, eager for a glimpse of the enemy, crept forward silently. They saw Adjutant Cowles point ahead and heard him speak quietly to his men.

"Right down there—get the range?" he said. "I think they're planting a battery."

Without warning, for there had been no previous firing, an enemy bullet whined through the air and struck the adjutant.

Putting his hand to his breast, the adjutant continued in the same quiet voice, "I got that in here." Then he slumped to the ground.

In another moment, enemy sharpshooters were raining bullets upon them all. The Yates battery poured return fire upon the spot to which the adjutant had pointed. Cord and George hurried back to get their own orders now that fighting had really started.

"I'm not afraid. I'm not afraid," Cord told himself fiercely as he ran, clenching his teeth to keep them from chattering.

During battle, the Drum Corps belonged to the Sanitary Commission and aided in getting the wounded off the field and to the hospital tents as quickly as possible. The huskier ones went forward as stretcher-bearers. Cord was detailed to follow them with water for the wounded.

A kind of Indian warfare continued all afternoon. Cord, racing back and forth from the spring with his load of canteens, quickly learned how to fall flat on his face for protection at the whine of a bullet or the shriek of a shell, then scramble up and run on when it had passed over. The distance back to the spring steadily grew, by which Cord knew they must be gaining. Time after time, he was shocked into speechlessness when he came upon a man whom he knew, lying bleeding and helpless, sometimes scarcely able to drink from the canteen when Cord held it to his lips.

Even in the midst of the horror, there were moments of relief. Once, on his way back to the spring with a load of canteens, Cord was trudging beside DeGraff when the shriek of a shell made them both fall on their faces. DeGraff stumbled and rolled over onto the big drum which was strapped to his back. He balanced on his head with his feet kicking wildly in the air until some of the men came to his rescue and set him right side up again. Cord doubled over with helpless laughter, laughter he couldn't seem to stop, until suddenly it choked him. He was standing near the battery where Adjutant Cowles had fallen, and not far from him was the adjutant's body, limp no longer as when Cord had seen it fall but stiff as the gun on the ground beside him.

Some officers of the Sanitary Commission approached, rolling a whiskey barrel over the littered ground. Cord watched, stupefied, fascinated, as they picked up the dead body of the adjutant and rammed it into the barrel, then carefully replaced the top. An army wagon drew up and the barrel was loaded onto it.

"Most of them stay here," one of the Sanitary Commission men said, "but he's to be sent home to his family. There's enough whiskey in the barrel to keep him."

"First casualty," the other man added. "He's due some deference."

"I think I'd rather be buried on the spot," Cord said.

The sanitary chief looked at him and smiled grimly. "These are things they don't tell you about when you enlist."

That night the Drum Corps set up their Sibley tent beside the Sanitary Commission. All about them were the tents of the temporary hospital, filled with groaning men, some of whom cried aloud with pain as the night wore on. Cord lay exhausted, staring into the darkness which veiled so much horror. He couldn't forget the queer limp look of the adjutant as he fell. A little way off he knew that many of his friends slept on their arms, ready for battle in the morning.

Soon after sunrise the firing began more aggressively than before, with an enemy battery training its guns upon the Tenth as the regiment was lined up for review. The Drum Corps, sixty paces behind the colors, stood its ground when the shells began to whistle overhead. They sounded the advance, then under Colonel Dickerson's orders fell back to the spring to await their work as stretcher-bearers and water carriers.

During those first two fighting days, the Michigan Tenth was a regiment in support and its encounters were considered to be sharp skirmishing. Whatever the words that described their actions, Cord thought, war was not the glorious thing he had imagined it would be; it was more like a monstrous bad dream.

Enemy firing stopped in the early afternoon of the second day as abruptly as it had commenced the day before. The Tenth continued in pursuit until nightfall, then camped several miles forward. In the morning they were told that they had successfully dislodged a line of enemy sharpshooters. They were then dispatched to a wooded ridge, an important point in the advance on Corinth, with orders to throw up earthworks and aid in maintaining the siege. The march that followed in torrid heat and through tropic swamps was a weary one, particularly since they had to lay their own road a good part of the way. When they reached the ridge, all men set to and dug furiously in the burning sun a long ditch eight to ten feet wide and four feet deep. The diggings they piled up in front for their protection, and settled in behind to keep watch over the enemy. Corinth was just visible in the distance and there the enemy was known to be.

Two days of desultory fighting followed. At dawn of the third day the men of the Union brigades were wakened by a long low rumbling sound coming from the direction of Corinth, then stillness; such stillness as there had not been since the shot rang through the air that had killed Adjutant Cowles.

Word soon came down the line that the enemy had evacuated and Corinth was empty. The retirement had been accomplished quietly in the night, all supplies having been transported. The long low rumbling sound came from their magazine, blown up on their departure.

The Michigan Tenth was retired to the town of Farmington where they camped in the main street. Camp Big Springs they called it. The men played ball on the common, swam in the creek, and had almost enough to eat; but Cord had lost all interest in such things. The days that followed were a miserable blur of heat and disappointment, a monotonous routine which he went through as one in a dream.

"Something's wrong with Little Foote," the men said.

"Aw, it's just the Tennessee quickstep that we've all got a touch of."

"He's too young for this kind of business. He ought to go home."

"He wouldn't go if you gave him a horse to ride all the way to Flint."

On a day in late June when the sun rode high in a quivering aura of humidity and thunderheads loomed on the horizon, Ira Miles came upon Cord sitting alone and dejected in the drummers' tent.

"Say, Cord," he said, "I know where there's some dandy blueberries. Come along and see."

They sauntered off together to the nearby woods where they scrambled about in the undergrowth, stirring up swarms of tiny insects, until each had filled his regimental cap with plump blueberries. Then they sat side by side on a fallen tree trunk and without words ate every berry. When they had finished, they just continued to sit there quietly for a time in the deep shade. The tiny insects sang about their ears and the distant thunder threatened. A little rabbit peeped out of the underbrush and scuttled past them. Cord thought of the baby rabbits he had left back home in April. They'd be big fellows by now, he decided. His guinea pigs, too. He thought about his banties and hoped somebody was taking care of them. Suddenly he realized that he had never been so miserable in all his life.

"You don't feel too good, do you, Cordie?" Ira Miles asked. Cord shook his head and put his hand on his stomach.

"I know," Ira said understandingly, "it's got us all and it's mighty uncomfortable, keeps a fellow on the run all the time. But it's nothing that won't wear away as soon as the hot weather lets up and we get more used to army rations." Then he flung a brotherly arm across Cord's shoulder. "You're awful homesick, ain't you, Cord?"

At which, quite unexpectedly, Cord began to cry. He cried and cried, like a calf bawling for its mother, and for once he didn't care who saw him.

Ira Miles sat quietly for a half hour or more until Cord got it out of his system, then he said, "You feel better now, don't you, Cord?"

The boy nodded.

Soon they started back to camp. Cord did feel better, much better, and those were the last tears he ever shed for himself.

CHAPTER III

A FEW DAYS LATER Cord encountered Captain Beach just after morning parade.

"How are you, Foote? I've been thinking you're not looking as fit as you should."

"Thank you, sir. I'm pretty good, sir." Cord's words had a briskness he was far from feeling. He didn't want Captain Beach to send him home. He felt he could endure anything if he might just stay on with his regiment.

"Well now, that's good." The captain was studying him. "But I don't like the look of you, Foote, and I want you to report to Dr. Sparling. He'll see that you're fixed up right."

Captain Beach scribbled something on a piece of paper and handed it to Cord. Cord went off reluctantly to the little group of tents, somewhat isolated from the rest, which served as regimental hospital. Dr. Sparling was busy with preparations for sending a number of his soldier patients with a wagon train to the divisional hospital at Hamburg Landing.

He read Captain Beach's note and looked clinically at Cord.

"You need better food than we can give you here for a while, boy. At Hamburg you can have that as well as a cot to sleep on. Food and rest, that's all you need, son; but you do need that pretty bad. Report to Lieutenant Colonel Dickerson for your Descriptive Roll, then come back here first thing tomorrow morning."

At regimental headquarters, Colonel Dickerson had a good deal to say as he signed Cord's roll which an orderly had prepared.

"I'm glad you're to have a change, Foote. If they can't fix you up at Hamburg Landing, go on to some place where they can—Cairo, or Jefferson Barracks. This paper is all you need to get you anywhere," he said, as he handed it to Cord. "You can go home with it, if you want to. The main thing is to get yourself fixed up. A sick man is no good to the army, you know. Quite the contrary. Now, take care of yourself, Foote, and don't come back till you're fit." He shook hands with him kindly. "Good-by, boy. Go right along home, if you've a mind to."

But that, Cord thought, was the last place he wanted to go. He clutched the paper tightly in his hands and went off to a quiet place at the edge of the camp to examine it carefully. He felt a surge of pride as he read the Descriptive Roll that proclaimed

> to all men by these presents that Coridon Edward Foote, age thirteen, color white, eyes blue, height four feet seven and a half inches, drummer boy for Company F, Tenth Michigan Infantry, United States Army, is a soldier in good standing to whom all courtesy is due, including at need both food and transportation, in witness whereof his commanding officers affix their signatures . . .

Those were words that proved he was a soldier, even

though he was being temporarily invalided out of the army.

Cord said good-by to his friends George Jay and Ira Miles. He handed his drum over to Old Lacey to keep for his return, but he tucked a pair of hickory sticks in his haversack so he could continue practicing what he had learned. With his slingshot in his pocket, he was ready to leave.

"Come back soon, Little Foote. We can't lick the Rebs without you," the men called after him.

The wagon train of disabled soldiers set off toward Hamburg Landing in the early morning, jolting painfully over the miles of rough corduroy road. Some of the soldiers in the wagons had helped construct the road when they had first gone south in the spring, felling the trees and sinking the logs in horizontal rows deep in the mud. Then, transport had been impossible without the crude foundation; but now the road lay like a bleaching skeleton under the burning sun. Many of the men, Cord among them, walked in the dust along the roadside all of the hot dry day. Fatigue was preferable to the jolting of the wagons.

At dusk they arrived at the divisional hospital, a large and miscellaneous collection of tents on the banks of the Tennessee River. Supper was waiting for them, and it was better food than many of the men had had since that memorable dinner given them by the ladies of Holly on the railway siding. There were cots to sleep on, as Dr. Sparling had said, and clean blankets too.

Cord was assigned to a ward in one of the tents. There he left his haversack and, as nothing was expected of him and no one seemed to care what he did, he spent his time roaming along the riverbank, watching the busy traffic on the broad expanse of the Tennessee. He ate three good meals a day; he slept soundly at night; and he began to feel better.

One day, as he was idling on the wharf watching the boats change cargoes, a big hospital boat drew up beside the landing. A number of soldiers, returning from points north, disembarked. Their places were soon taken by men requiring treatment at better-equipped hospitals farther from the front. Watching them, Cord became possessed with a desire to go along with them, wherever the boat might be going.

He approached the officer in charge at the gangplank and presented his Descriptive Roll. The officer examined it cursorily, then more carefully.

"What's the matter, Bub, getting tired of it around here so soon?"

"No, sir, but I haven't been feeling very good."

"Think you'd feel better boat riding, eh?" The officer grinned.

Cord grinned back. "Yes, sir, I'm sure I would."

Another officer came up and the two drew aside for consultation. Cord tried to act as if he didn't know they were talking about him. After what seemed an unnecessarily long time, the first officer returned and, smiling, handed back his Descriptive Roll.

"All right, sonny, climb on."

When the big boat drew off and turned down the Tennessee toward the Ohio, Cord did not know where it was going, nor did he care. It was pleasant on the river and he liked the stir of life aboard the steamer. Four days later, when the boat turned upstream on the Mississippi, Cord began to think of his destination. Men all about him were talking of Jefferson Barracks. Lieutenant Colonel Dickerson had spoken of Jefferson Barracks. Cord decided that he would get off there.

He was pleased at his decision when, at sundown the next day, he caught his first glimpse of the barracks. Set among trees high on a wooded bluff were two parallel rows of one-story buildings which faced each other across a parade ground. At one end, the buildings were linked by a two-story row which looked out upon the broad Mississippi. Looking comfortable, quiet and well-groomed, Jefferson Barracks seemed remote from the junglelike forests and war-torn crossroads of the region around Corinth and Hamburg Landing.

A group of officers and their ladies in gay summer dress sat laughing and talking on an upper veranda. They watched the men from the hospital boat as they were unloaded, then marched or were carried across the parade ground to the hospital wards. Cord brought up the rear. As a drummer boy he should have led the straggling band, but his drum was back with his regiment where he knew he would be before long.

Dr. Van Dyne, a genial young man, assigned Cord to Ward H as a convalescent. Cord slept in a real bed that night, and the next day he sat down at a real table for his meals, and he ate real butter and fresh meat. Among the privileges that had been given him was the freedom of the Post, and his time was his own. After two or three days a messenger came to tell him that Dr. Fish, the head surgeon, wished to speak with him at his residence.

Cord looked puzzled. Why should a doctor want to see him when he was feeling better every day?

"Them's orders," the steward urged. He cocked his head across the parade ground to the upper veranda where Cord had seen the gaily dressed ladies and their officer escorts the day he arrived. "Don't be scared, boy. The doctor's wife, she's a grand lady."

Cord trudged across the parade ground, conscious of his soiled and baggy trousers and unkempt army blouse. The veranda was reached by an outside stairway at the rear, and all too soon he found himself in the open doorway with the eyes of the gathered company upon him. He was not certain whether he should salute or not, but decided to risk it, and delivered his best salute with long-practiced military precision.

"Aye, aye, sir!" was the jovial response of a tall, fine-looking man in light uniform who advanced toward him. "Are you Coridon Edward Foote? Long name for a short lad like you."

"They call me 'Cord' for short, sir."

Everybody laughed and Cord felt a little more at ease.

"You're from Flint, aren't you, Cord? Know that young fellow over there?" The man in light uniform indicated a tall youth leaning over the back of a chair. He advanced to shake hands with Cord eagerly.

"Hello, Cordie. How in the name of heaven did you get here?"

It was George Fish, who lived scarcely a block away in Flint. He had enlisted from his college and was now serving with his uncle at the Post.

Before Cord could answer, the doctor's wife said, "Sit down, Cord, and be comfortable, and tell us your adventures. I know you've had lots of them."

Cord thought he had never seen anyone quite so beautiful, and with all her air of the fine lady she had managed in a few words to make him feel completely at home. Then all the ladies began to ask him questions—how had he got into the army? What was life like at the front?

Cord felt as if he talked more in that one evening than in all his thirteen years.

When tattoo sounded and Cord got up to go, Dr. Fish said to him, "Foote, Dr. Van Dyne and I think you'll be happier around here if you have something to do, and we have a fine job for you."

He explained that the kitchen of the residence was in the basement of a corner building toward the river, which made a three-story climb for their servingmaid in bringing food up to the dining room. Cord was detailed to give assistance between the kitchen and the residence.

"You'll get lots of good things to eat, Cord, if you're up and at it, and kind to the cook. We've got the best cook in the country, you'll see for yourself. And you'll be like the Irishman who got a job carrying bricks to the top of a new building. He wrote back home and said, 'This is a foine country, Pat, all I got to do is carry the bricks up four stories, and the fellow at the top does all the wurruk.'"

Amid the laughter that followed, Cord said good night and went back to his ward feeling as pleased with himself as he was with life in general.

The Negro cook took a liking to Cord and fed him well with her choicest southern cookery. Mrs. Fish saw that Cord had a new uniform, and a well-fitting one this time; also a change of clothing, and other modest luxuries. One of the nurses taught him to dance. With George Fish he explored the river and the nearby woods, and under his tutelage became fairly adept at checkers and chess. Cord grew plump and robust, even a little taller. He found there was plenty to write home about. War had become again the glorified Sunday school picnic it had started out to be, not the monstrous bad dream.

Then Dr. Fish was ordered to an eastern post. Cord had to say good-by to him and to Mrs. Fish, and to the friendly cook.

"It's the fortunes of war, Cord," Dr. Van Dyne said consolingly.

Dr. Groves, now head surgeon at Jefferson Barracks, had a glass eye, a disagreeable temper, and a mania for discipline. Under him, life at the Post assumed an altered aspect. After a few days of wondering what he would do with himself, Cord received a summons to report to Dr. Groves.

"Foote," the doctor said abruptly, "they tell me you are

just the kind of boy I want in my office—to keep things swept and dusted up, and be ready for messenger duty when I need you. I'll expect you to take care of my instruments, too. When we hold a post-mortem at the Dead House, I want you to bring the instruments down there. Afterward you'll be responsible for cleaning them up and putting them back in place here at the office. This is very important. Can I depend on you, Foote?"

"Yes, sir." Cord brought his hand to his forehead in salute.

The next three weeks were spent mainly in the doctor's office and at the Dead House. There seemed to be a post-mortem practically every day, and Cord abhorred his gruesome task as custodian of the bloodstained surgical instruments; but it was his military duty to wash and polish them, place them in their heavy cases and carry the cases back to Dr. Groves' office.

Relief appeared for him in the visits of two ladies from St. Louis who came to the Post every Thursday with baskets of pastries and sweets for the convalescent soldiers. Cord was detailed to meet them at the train and carry their baskets for them. One looked so like his sister Hannah that it made him feel good just to see her, and the ladies always had something special for him. Relief from the Dead House was also found in the company of two sporting stewards who allowed Cord to help them every evening in the business of making nets to snare quail.

One October day the three of them went on a hunting expedition. The woods were in their autumn regalia and game was abundant. They brought to bag a fine lot of quail, which they cooked and ate before returning to the Post that night.

When Cord reported at the office in the morning, Dr. Groves was in a temper.

"Foote, where were you yesterday afternoon? I needed

you, and I needed you bad. We'll have no foolishness now, young man."

"I was out after quail, Dr. Groves, and say, I got some beauties!"

The doctor glared at him with his one eye, then continued, "I tell you I needed you bad. Quail!" he snorted. "Out after quail, and got some beauties, did you? I'll make you quail—"

He launched into a harangue about the need for military discipline at the Post. Cord stood at attention all through it.

"I'll let you off this time," the doctor concluded grouchily, "but no more hunting trips, young man, hear me?" Dr. Groves leaned back in his chair and picked up a report that was lying on his desk.

"Yes, sir. Please, sir—"

"Well, what is it now?"

Cord had recently been on messenger duty and knew that many men were soon to be sent back to their regiments. "Excuse me, sir, but don't you think I'm fit enough now to go back to my regiment?"

The doctor looked up in surprise. "What!" he shouted. "You don't mean you're asking to go back to the front?"

"Yes, sir. I want to go back to my regiment."

Dr. Groves lost his belligerent tone and became almost fatherly as he spoke of the advantages of the comfortable life at the Post.

Cord listened, respectful but unconvinced. "Yes, sir, that's all true, but my place is with my regiment."

The doctor glared at him with his good eye and growled something about the "slaughter of the innocents" and the "pigheaded presumption of upstart minors" and the "criminal irresponsibility of those who were letting them into the army." Then he said, "Well, if you're set on going back, I'll put your name down."

Without waiting to thank him, Cord rushed out upon the parade ground, where the men scheduled for return were gathered.

"Boys," he shouted, "I'm going back to my regiment!"

His exultation was infectious and though some of the men were far from jubilant over their own return, they gave Cord a cheer as he raced across to Ward H to get his belongings and put them in his haversack.

The first lap of his journey took him to St. Louis by the little branch railroad which had always brought the good ladies with their sweets. Here Cord waited several days for transportation, eating where he could and sleeping at the "Soldiers' Home," an abandoned warehouse near the docks which afforded by way of shelter little more than walls and cobweb-draped roof. When the steamer *Tigris* was ready to depart for Memphis, a swarm of returning soldiers crowded aboard, Cord among them, and the second lap of the journey began.

Once clear of the city harbor, the late-autumn magic of the Mississippi was all about them. For hours at a time the *Tigris*, a big boat with a reputation for speed, plied along the mirrorlike expanse of the river, trailing twin plumes of black smoke and leaving a fanlike wake of ruffled water that spread and spread until it blotted out the quiet reflection of the vivid-hued trees that lined both banks. At the many ports of call she added her clamor to the stir of river traffic—rafts, boats and barges, their wakes interweaving until the water surface was crisscrossed and checked and mottled with their movement and the air was loud with the shrill and throaty calling that came from the different pilots.

Leaving one of the ports, the *Tigris* came abreast of her rival, the *Lily Belle*, a boat which had recently taken from the *Tigris* the laurels for speed which she had held so long. Some of the crew bellowed a challenge, and the two boats were off on a wild day's race with Cairo for goal. Cord was one with the crazy excitement of it, matching as it did his own impatience to get back to his regiment.

For a long time the two big boats, Ohio bound, ran beside each other. Whatever loss or gain was made at ports of call, it was soon wiped out when they reached the open river again. The passengers crowded to the near rails, cheering wildly. As the day wore on, the *Tigris* began to drop behind. Her captain ordered the passengers from the starboard rail, telling them to keep center for the sake of easier steering. When the *Tigris* began to gain by this measure, the rival captain was quick to imitate it and the *Lily Belle* forged ahead.

With boats so well matched, victory depended upon the strength of stokers and the skill of pilots. Cord, feeling that he had more to gain than anyone else on board from the outcome of the race, rushed frantically from pilothouse to hold. Between the two, the passengers milled about shouting taunts and advice, and betting recklessly. In the stokers' hold, six sweating Negroes, bare to the waist, shoveled soft coal under the boilers. When the fires seemed to lag for a moment, they poured on pitch from huge barrels, singing and swearing as they coaxed the flames. Up in the pilothouse, a tall, whiskered steersman stood to the wheel, scarcely lifting his eyes from the river ahead, while two husky young assistants took turns at helping him "pull her down," silent, eager, intent.

When there were still perhaps two hours to go, the *Tigris* was lagging almost five lengths behind. The stokers had begun to tap the barrels of pitch reserved for the final effort. As much flame as smoke belched from the tall chimneys, and stewards played streams of water on the deck to keep the sparks that were showering down from igniting. The *Tigris* strained to the utmost. Her captain thought to gain by skipping a port of call, but his watchful rival perceived his intention and, swinging the *Lily Belle* about, soon took the lead again. From that time on, it was just a steady, heartbreaking pull for Cairo with the *Tigris* three lengths behind.

Then a passenger who had come aboard the *Tigris* that morning with a load of pine knots made the princely offer of some of his resin wood for a final spurt of speed. Passengers cheered him roundly as they fell to with the crew toting pine knots to the stokers' hold. Soon, fire belched from the chimneys more furiously than before, sparks swirled fiercely and streams of water were played on the deck for safety. Below, the stokers hurled in more pine knots with their shovels of coal and poured on floods of pitch. Fires roared and men shouted crazily as the *Tigris* slowly pulled ahead.

When the harbor of Cairo came into view, she was so far in the lead that her pilot dared to cut across the bows of the *Lily Belle* for inside way. The *Tigris* steamed into port in a frenzy of whistling and bell ringing, while the passenger who had given the pine knots had the honor of nailing a broom to the fore of the pilothouse in token of laurels regained.

At Cairo, the *Tigris* put up for the night to recuperate and change cargo. Cord, feeling that he was that much nearer to his regiment, watched the men of the *Tigris* prepare to celebrate their victory. Collecting their winnings from the day's betting, they went off to one of the waterfront saloons. At first Cord thought he would like to go with them; later when they returned, having lost most of what they had won, he was glad of the promise he had made to his mother not to gamble.

The *Tigris* left the next morning for Columbus, Kentucky, where Cord expected to get a train for Farmington. When he showed his roll to an officer at Columbus, he inquired about his regiment and learned that the Tenth was now with the Army of the Cumberland near Nashville.

"You'll have to go back downriver to Cairo, sonny, then get a train to New Albany, Indiana. Once there, you can cross by ferry to Louisville and get a train to Nashville."

Cord folded the paper that was becoming worn from much showing. After the speed on the river, it seemed a long and weary way he would have to go before he would be with his friends.

It took him three days to get to the Louisville and Nashville Railway, then in as many hours the train ran into trouble. Morgan's Raiders had been at Nicholasville, halfway down the line, and had set fire to a train of boxcars into which they had put oil-soaked and inflammable material. They had run the train into the long tunnel that began near Nicholasville, and the flaming boxcars ignited supporting timbers and caused a serious cave-in. The train with its passengers went back to Louisville, except for ten soldiers among whom was Cord. They decided to go by foot the twenty-five miles to the other end of the tunnel.

A young sergeant took command and the ten kept close together. It was hard going and dangerous, for the region was alive with guerrillas. Up the wild mountain they went, through dense cedar forest and over the rocky height, until the early November dusk closed in about them. A chill rain was falling. They could not get a fire to burn so they slept on the wet ground with their blankets for protection. In the morning they woke stiff with cold and exposure. Added to their difficulties was thick fog which had settled into the mountains during the night and through which they would have to grope their way. They breakfasted on hardtack and some chestnuts they found. Scrambling down the eastern face of the mountain, they hoped to reach the other end of the tunnel by nightfall, but dusk came upon them by midafternoon.

Another fireless night, another foggy morning, and at last they reached the tunnel mouth. Fortunately for them, a train was waiting there and it carried them to Nashville within a few hours. It was seven days since Cord had left Columbus, and he was not yet with his regiment.

He spent the night in comparative comfort at the Zollicopher House, an unfinished hotel which had been turned into a crude Soldiers' Home. Cord asked one soldier after another as to the whereabouts of the Tenth, but received only conflicting reports. After two days he obtained a definite clue. The Tenth had been sent on a guard march to Stone's River. With the other lodgers at the Zollicopher House, Cord fortified himself with a breakfast of coffee and bacon cooked over an outside fire, then he set forth briskly and alone on the Owensville Pike.

There was a breathless, excited feeling inside him as he thought that soon he would be with the boys of the Tenth again. Nothing could stop him now. He was on the way to Stone's River and that was less than a day's march.

It was a crisp clear morning and as he crested one long hill after another of the beautiful old road he was following, he could see many miles ahead of him to where the highway lost itself in a far blue rim of surrounding mountains. By noon, he was a good halfway on his course when he saw in the distance, coming toward him, a considerable wagon train. Topping the next hill, he saw that it had come much nearer, and he found his steps hastening in the hope of gaining more definite news of his regiment. By the time he reached the next hilltop, he could look down directly on the approaching train. An infantry guard marched ahead and alongside and the lumbering wagons with their plodding mule teams filled the road as far as he could see, trailing up and over the hill beyond.

The vanguard was distant by only some two hundred yards from him when Cord, descending the hill which they were climbing, thought he recognized one of the men of the Tenth. He quickened his step. Hardly an instant later, someone recognized him.

"Hi, boys," came the shout, "there's Little Foote!"

The cry was taken up and repeated along the line.

"By golly, it's Little Foote up the road there!"

"Little Foote's comin' there, fellows!"

"Hell, men, it's the boy himself!"

With tingling ears, Cord heard them. The welcome grew into jubilation, halting the wagons nearest them as the men surrounded Cord and pumped his right arm joyously. George Jay hammered him like a brother. Old Lacey embraced him like a father.

"Bless you, boy, I mighta known you'd never say die."

An officer rode up to investigate the delay. Seeing Cord he gave him a friendly welcome. The men began to cheer Cord. They were still cheering, farther back along the line, as the wagons at the fore resumed their laborious way. Cord trudged with them back again up the hill he had just come down, happier than he had been for a long time.

CHAPTER IV

CORD FELT FIT, and every inch a veteran. He was ready for the battle for which he had been waiting, but not for the trouble in which he soon became involved.

Winter set in early with a six-inch snowfall, followed by weeks of cruel cold. Snow or not, the Michigan Tenth was detailed for another guard march from Stone's River to Nashville and return. On the morning of the storm, Cord was wakened by Old Lacey to drum reveille in the first gray light of dawn. Orders were given to be ready to march in ten minutes. This would have been impossible in the earlier days, but the luggage with which they had first set out had been carefully reduced. Chief among the reductions was the replacement of their clumsy Sibley tents by small squares of canvas known as pup tents. These were finished on three sides with buttons and buttonholes, and when fastened together and swung over a new-cut ridgepole set in two crotched sticks made a tent which would shelter six men.

On the march, each man carried his own square of canvas with his blankets rolled up inside.

Striking camp, and setting up camp again at the end of a march, had now become an open contest to determine the six tentmates who were most efficient. On that particular morning, Cord's group of drummers had the satisfaction of finishing a full minute before any other group. They lined up before the waiting wagon train and commenced tapping out the Common Time march.

Old Lacey shook his head at the sound. "It's the cold that does it, and the dampness. Release your snares, boys, and you'll get a tone that's less flabby."

While the drummers worked over their drums, Pop Lacey kept up the march, quickening the time. When the boys picked up their sticks again and sounded off, he listened. Then he nodded. "That's better, but the cold is in your fingers as well. Let them have it now, boys. It's up to you to make the men want to march."

The drummers put their hearts into their hands. The tapping became more brisk. It rolled up into the raw cold of the dark morning, cutting through it with a surge of sound. Men started marching, wagon wheels turned, hoofs dug into the snow-softened ground, and the supply train plodded on toward Nashville.

During the day the low-hanging clouds dissolved into thick-driven snow that blinded the marching men and wet them through as it melted and ran down their necks and soaked through the cracked leather of their boots. The rutted road became a slippery clay mire, all but impassable. They struggled through it doggedly, while the muleteers laughed and shouted and swore and called to the men to lend a hand in desperate places. It was nearly midnight when they reached Nashville. Some of the men were sobbing with cold and exhaustion, their clothes frozen stiff upon them as a keen, clear night followed the day's wet snowfall.

Orders came to make camp near Cherry Creek, just outside the city, where a score or more of abandoned Sibley tents stood in ghostly array in the moonlight. Within this scanty shelter, the men of the Michigan Tenth spread the canvas of their pup tents on the ground and rolled up in their blankets. They were so tired that they felt numb to both cold and hunger.

The next day was taken up with foraging for firewood. The constant need for wood had used up all the legitimate fuel and the men had to go considerable distances into the surrounding countryside to obtain any wood worth burning. Cord discovered an admirable source of supply and with two of his fellow drummers made a foray upon a neighboring cemetery fence built of eight-foot cedar poles three or four inches thick, set close together in a trench and bound at the top with withes. It was an hour's hard work to get out even a few of the poles, but they were beautifully seasoned for burning.

The boys had furnished several groups of soldiers with wood for their fires when they were apprehended by the corporal's guard and led to regimental headquarters on a charge of stealing.

"You boys ought to be ashamed of yourselves," Lieutenant Colonel Dickerson said when informed of their depredations. "I know you're cold, but not cold enough to justify robbing the dead. Why, I could have you fellows hung up by the thumbs for a felony, and I've a great mind to do it, too, if you're not good and plenty sorry for the disgraceful thing you've done."

He talked on for ten minutes, growing more and more scathing in his condemnation of their misdemeanor. Then his tone changed abruptly. "I'll let you boys off this time with three days in the guardhouse, but mind—no more robbing of the dead!"

As they trudged off toward the wretched hut that served for guardhouse, Cord felt frightened and ashamed. He also felt defiant. They had been so miserably cold. What did the dead care about the old fence anyway! Hurrying footsteps could be heard behind them and the boys turned to face the corporal's guard.

"Foote, report back to Colonel Dickerson at once."

Cord forgot both shame and defiance as he retraced his steps. He was desperately frightened. The idea of dismantling the cemetery fence had been his in the first place. Perhaps Colonel Dickerson knew that and was going to give him a stiffer sentence.

Standing before Colonel Dickerson, Cord saluted and waited for his sentence.

"All right, Foote, you go back to drummers' quarters and see that you behave yourself." Colonel Dickerson turned away and directed his attention to the papers on his desk.

Cord went toward the door, but he could not open it. The relief that he felt was overcome by a sense of fairness to his fellow drummers.

"What's the matter, son, rather go to the guardhouse?"

Cord's eyes blazed as he swung around to face his commanding officer. "It was me that started it, sir," he burst forth.

Colonel Dickerson looked at him with an odd gleam in the gray eyes under their shaggy brows. "It was, eh?" He was silent for a moment. "Well, you know better now. Go back to your tent and behave yourself, I say."

Cord did go back. After one night he was joined by his fellows, who had been paroled from the guardhouse.

Guard duty at the base of supplies was a monotonous routine. As the December days moved on, each one colder than the last, the only enemy the Tenth seemed to be facing was the winter.

"I wish we'd hurry up and have a battle to write home about," Cord lamented one night as he and George Jay and Ira Miles crouched sociably about a single candle set on top of a wooden box on which their sheets of camp paper were spread as they tried to write letters home. It was a night of thick fog and foreboding silence; silence only accentuated by the long-drawn rumblings of heavily loaded freight trains laboring up from Louisville to discharge their cargoes and soon to rattle past again as empties.

Cord chewed the end of his pen for inspiration.

"Aw, tell 'em how you got arrested, Footey," teased George Jay. "That'll get 'em more excited than a battle."

Cord flushed.

"Lay off o' the young'un!" came threateningly from Ira Miles. "Never mind, Cordie, he's just mad because he never got arrested."

"Mad, your granny! Think I want to be shut up in that stinkin' guardhouse? But it's dead sure I am that if I did get arrested they'd never think I was too sweet and tender to do my time."

"And you're dead right," Cord countered. "They'd lock you up for life!"

The Michigan Tenth was now a unit of the First Brigade, Second Division, Fourteenth Army Corps, lately designated the Army of the Cumberland, with General Rosecrans in command. Erect and soldierly, in full panoply of gold braid and tasseled saber, the general was a gallant figure as he sat his handsome gray horse on his twice-weekly visits to the Tenth. These were occasions when the Drum Corps outdid themselves as they beat the different calls on the parade ground and signaled maneuvers. General Rosecrans, Old Rosy as the men called him, was courteous and kindly and greatly loved; though the men could on occasions smart under his discipline, they respected him for it.

One day, at dress parade, the drummers were required to do a long roll with muffled drums while a young officer, whom they all knew well, was sharply reprimanded by General Rosecrans and formally reduced to the ranks. This was discipline. The officer, doing picket duty on one of the highways approaching Nashville, had become tired of his detail, for nothing ever seemed to happen. He had posted his men and gone off to Nashville to enjoy himself on the very afternoon that General Rosecrans and his staff rode by, inquiring for the officer on guard.

"Absent without authority" was the pronouncement, as the officer stood at attention before the general while his epaulets were cut from his shoulders.

Cord was not the only one who burned with shame.

Discipline came to be increasingly needed as day after uneventful day passed by with all too much leisure for the six thousand men on guard at the base of supplies. Reveille sounded at five o'clock in the morning, the regiment stood in battle formation for an hour of inspection after breakfast; then there was nothing to do until dress parade in the evening. The men had the freedom of the city, and they made use of it. Gambling and drunkenness were rife. The camp was overrun with bootleggers, mostly women, who came in the pretense of bringing hot chicken soup to the soldiers but whose real errand was the sale of mountain moonshine, which they carried in bottles hooked under their spreading crinolines. Cord made frequent trips to the city to get papers to sell to the men. Old Lacey and Ira Miles kept their eyes on him to make sure that he did not become involved in any way with the bootleggers; but innate decency and that promise to his mother which was as faithfully kept as it was fervently given preserved Cord.

Partial compensation for the dullness of duty at the base camp was the good food they had. The drummers rattled out the various calls for mess with an enthusiasm they had found lacking when hardtack and salt beef were all that could be offered. Peas on a Trencher, the traditional call for breakfast, was sounded with good will; but the drummers put real zest into the dinner call, Roast Beef, especially when Wardie Fisher was serving pork and beans.

Wardie had been cook in a Michigan lumber camp. Company F, with him for cook, was the envy of the division. When Wardie found that pork and beans would be rationed for a time, he enlisted the aid of the Drum Corps to scour town and countryside for bake kettles. They got busy and rounded up enough iron cauldrons, some of them three feet across, for Wardie to furnish the men with a daily feast of ground-baked beans.

Cord's part in the hunt for kettles took him two miles up Cherry Creek to a lonely house back from the road, where he found an old lady making cherry pies. She welcomed his Yankee uniform, for her own son was fighting in the Union army. Cord spent the morning in her warm, fragrant kitchen, eating all of a big cherry pie. Before he left, he had bargained with her for two more pies which he carried back to camp, selling them for twice as much as he had paid for them. It became a thriving business among the old lady, Cord, and the men of the Tenth. Two or three times a week he would trudge the two miles up Cherry Creek with an empty basket and return with it filled with pies.

Christmas was drawing near. The days grew darker and drearier. The cold continued. Neither cherry pie, nor moonshine, nor Wardie's baked beans could content the men with the slow progress of things. People in Nashville said that the armies of the North and South had settled into the nearby mountains and were doing nothing but glare at each other.

The men of the Tenth, nerves edgy with idleness, felt that they had no one to glare at but their own messmates. To make a new friend those days was often an occasion.

"It's good to see the likes of you," Sergeant Branch, a big blustering Irishman of Company I, said to Cord one day. "Ye know, lad, ye always remind me of the little feller at home."

To Cord, that was faint praise. Back in Flint, Tommy Branch was one of the small boys that he could think of only with condescension.

"Thank you, sir," Cord said, glad to know in any case that he had a friend in Sergeant Branch.

Cord and George Jay often went on hunting expeditions into the surrounding countryside, bagging with their slingshots small game which Cord carried back to camp in his drum. Unloosing the ropes so he could remove the batter head and put the game in his drum was a tedious process, but Cord discovered a trick that made it easily possible. George Jay often wearied waiting for Cord to lace his drum up again, but Cord said that if it took an hour he was going to get their game back to Wardie for supper without having to surrender it to a sentry.

George Jay sighed and waited. Time was the one thing they had that winter.

Whenever they were hunting, Cord was constantly on the lookout for some unusual bird to send back to his mother for his collection at home. But often, seeing one, he had to let it go. There was no use bagging one unless he knew of someone returning to Michigan to whom he could entrust it.

In their ramblings the boys began to be joined by a fifteen-year-old lad of the Illinois 68th Artillery. His name was Jimmie Tyson, but he was called Sissie for his curly golden hair and peach-blown complexion. However, there was nothing sissy about Jimmie, as Cord and George soon discovered. He was quick of eye and hand, a sure shot with the sling, and always venturesome. Late one afternoon they were turning back to camp, thoroughly satisfied with their day's adventure, when they saw a man in faded blue scramble out of a ravine just ahead of them and run for cover in a cedar brake down the rugged slope toward the road.

The boys followed him silently. When he broke from cover again, Cord and George recognized him as a man from their own regiment.

"By golly, it's Malachi!" Cord whispered.

"The fellow you said used to bring you butter an' eggs back home?"

"Yea, an' so cranky he don't even know me down here. What d'you s'pose he's up to?"

They picked their way in stealthy pursuit until they saw him break for the road below.

"Well, if you want to know what I think," drawled George Jay, "I think he's makin' another run for the butter an' eggs back home."

They followed to the edge of the embankment and peered down along the road from the sheltering screen of cedars.

"You mean he's desertin'?"

"I guess that's the name for it, Cordie. They say he's been caught at it twice already."

"Gosh, it'll go hard with him if they get him this time!" Sissie exclaimed.

Malachi had vanished into the woods on the other side of the road, but at almost the same moment two riders in blue appeared around a bend in the road.

"Say! There was a narrow squeak. What'll you bet those pickets saw him?"

The boys stood still as they heard the familiar creaking and jangle of wagons coming along the road. Presently, three well-loaded wagons of a forage train appeared, with six big horses straining before each and a plodding guard of Yankee infantry surrounding them. The boys turned away to go back to camp.

Suddenly two shots rang out, fired by the men who rode in advance.

"Take cover," Sissie whispered hoarsely.

The three boys lay flat in the bushes. The sound of trampling hoofs coming up the road could be heard, and in another moment all was confusion of yelling and swearing, close firing, slashing with sabers, as a score of enemy cavalry swooped down upon the toiling train. Two horses were shot from under the leaders of the charge, but the riders scrambled free and succeeded in intercepting the rear wagon of the train. They jerked the horses to a halt and partly turned them around before they were charged by some infantrymen of the Yankee guard. These, in turn, were surrounded by enemy cavalry and swept along down the road as prisoners. Meanwhile, two other cavalrymen succeeded in loosing from the frightened rear team four of the horses, then stampeded them down the steep slope up which they had just laboriously climbed with their load. The shots of the Yankee infantrymen rained after them.

It was over in a few breathless moments, and the last of the enemy cavalry rode on with three wounded across their saddles. The demoralized remnant of the Yankee guard struggled awhile to right the rear wagon, then they brought horses from the wagon in front, gathered up their few wounded and laid them in the wagons, and patiently resumed their plodding way.

"There's a battle for you to write home about, Cordie," said George.

"Cripes, but those Johnnies are fast workers! Five prisoners, six wounded, two horses captured in about five minutes," Sissie said admiringly.

"Sure, but what about two horses killed, an' the four Johnnies wounded, an' the good old forage train all safe an' sound?" Cord defended.

In the excitement of it all and the stress of getting back the five miles to camp before dress parade, Malachi was forgotten. But late that night, orders came to the Drum Corps from Colonel Dickerson to be ready to sound an early reveille. There was to be an execution at sunrise. A deserter had been captured in his third attempt.

"Gosh, that must be Malachi!" Cord exclaimed, and he felt himself turn rigid with horror.

Some of the Drum Corps flamed with rebellion at so sharp a sentence, but Old Lacey sprang to the defense of discipline. That sort of thing must be stopped, he said, or there'd be no army left at the base of supplies. It was scandalous the way the fellows were dropping out. Three had disappeared only yesterday. Somebody had to be made an example of, and Malachi happened to be the unlucky fellow. That was the way of war.

Cord could think only of the old lady who used to come with Malachi on his rounds. She would sit on the high seat of the wagon holding the horses while Malachi went to the door with his wares. She had often told Cord what a good son her boy was. One day, while Cord patted the horses, she said she hoped he would grow up to be as kind and good to his mother as Malachi had always been to her. Cord hoped he would never have to see her again. It was one thing, he thought, to be shot in battle; it was very much something else to be stood up and fired at in cold blood by the men of your own regiment just because you got tired of things and tried to go home. Cord said as much to Old Lacey.

"Where'd the army be, Cordie, I'd like to know, if the rest of us took a notion to go home? We've just as big a right to. I tell you fellows this is *war*, and we've got to stay by and do as we're told, even if we just sit around here and freeze for another year."

There was little sleep for Cord that night as he shivered in his blanket and waited for Old Lacey's call. Thinking of what he had seen . . . of what he had remembered . . . and of what Old Lacey had said . . . he prayed that he would never want to go home like Malachi, never want to go at all until he had a right to. He was still shivering when Old Lacey dragged him out before dawn. He kept on shaking with dread and horror as he marched down the Sallywhite Pike with the other drummers.

When the regiment reached a large open field they turned into it and formed a hollow square as the drummers beat the slow march with muffled drums. One side of the square was left open and through it Malachi was drawn, seated on his coffin which was mounted on a gun limber. A priest walked beside him. Six of the firing squad marched before the gun limber, and six behind. The squad had been chosen by lot from the regiment and was supplied with cartridges of which half were blank. No one would ever know who fired the fatal shot. The small procession halted beside a freshly dug grave.

The black-robed priest prayed with the prisoner for a few minutes while the muffled drums continued. Then he helped Malachi down from his coffin which was drawn a little to the side. The priest first, then Colonel Dickerson, shook hands with Malachi. The corporal's guard stepped up to blindfold him. The drums were silenced. The members of the firing squad took their places.

"Ready on your marks!" the sharp order rang out. "Aim! Fire!"

The twelve guns crashed. Malachi threw up his arms and fell over backward.

Cord closed his eyes. It was a terrible thing to see a man fall beside his own coffin, close to his own grave.

"Four bullets through the heart, two about six inches from the heart," he heard someone say.

That afternoon Cord wandered alone in downtown Nashville. He couldn't get Malachi out of his mind and he was afraid someone would guess how downright sick the whole thing had made him. He didn't care much, just then, what became of him. Promises made to his mother seemed to belong to an unreal world, so far away that he doubted if he would ever see it again. He was lonely, lonelier than he had ever been since the Michigan Tenth had laughed and sung its way out of Flint almost a year ago. Malachi had been in one of those lumbering wagons, laughing and singing. The people lining the street had cheered him as much as any of the other soldiers. And now—Cord rubbed his eyes. But nothing could take away the picture he had seen that morning.

Uncertain what to do, where to go, sure only that he wanted to forget but that he could not, he loitered in an alley. He could smell savory odors from the half-open door of a restaurant kitchen and he wondered dully if he would ever want to eat again.

Suddenly the door was opened wide and a bundle of something alive came hurtling out and dropped almost at his feet. The door slammed to, cutting short a man's angry oath, and the bundle straightened itself into a ragged little black dog, half-stunned and whimpering. In an instant Cord was on his knees, his feet in the gutter, with the little dog shivering in his arms as he tried to comfort it. Presently he drew from his pocket a chunk of bread and some bacon which the dog devoured in two starved gulps.

They raced back to camp together and Cord introduced

his new friend to the Drum Corps, beginning with Old Lacey.

"He can share my bed and eat my food," Cord said defiantly. "We're both small."

One look at Cord's face, at the blue eyes that were so staring-big, had been enough for Old Lacey to know what the dog had done for the boy who had been devastated by the morning's duty. He assured Cord that the little dog would have full rights in the Drum Corps, but that he must have a name.

"Chris," one of the men called out, "for isn't this pretty close to Christmas Eve and isn't he the only present we're like to be getting?"

The men cheered and Cord hugged Chris to him.

Other men had drifted into the tent and were indulging in some sentimental memories of Christmas back home when the tent flap was drawn up and a small boy stood in the opening, blinking in the candlelight. The boy looked wan and weary. No one recognized him except Sergeant Branch, who thought for a moment that he must be the ghost of the son he had left back home.

"Holy Mother, spare us!" was all Big Tom could gasp out.

"Hello, Tommy!" Cord exclaimed, as he realized who it was. Clutching his dog to him, he went toward the small boy and stared at him.

"Tommy Branch," the sergeant said, "I do believe it's you!"

"Sure it is," Tommy protested, "an' I tells yuh me mother sent me to mail a letter to yuh fer Chrismus, an' thinks I, if the letter kin git there fer Chrismus so kin I. I gits a ride to Holly, an' I climbs on a freight train, an' I gits here fer Chrismus."

"Santy Claus must have brought you to your pa the way he brought Chris to me," Cord said, grinning with delight and quite forgetful of the fact that Tommy had once seemed too young for him. Now there would be someone in the regiment near his own size.

Tommy smiled for the first time, sure of his welcome.

"Big Tom's boy has come to see him!" The word ran through the camp and soon the tent was not big enough to hold all the men who wanted to crowd into it. Setting Tommy on his shoulders, Sergeant Branch led the way to Company F's mess tent and soon Wardie Fisher was serving hot coffee and pie as a Christmas celebration.

The next day, from early morning on, there was cold driving rain; and from early morning, all through the day, there was the steady tramp of regiment after regiment sloshing along the road to Stone's River. Plainly something crucial was pending. Cord watched it all, somberly, from his tent, with Chris held fast in his arms. He had made a collar for Chris from an old gun strap, and a leash from clothesline begged from the Sanitary Commission. Chris was equipped as a member of Company F, Tenth Michigan Infantry.

Late in the day, Sergeant Branch came to ask the Drum Corps to take care of Tommy. The sergeant had been detailed with fifteen men from Company I to hold a stockade at an important railway trestle ten miles out. "And that's no place for a little tyke," Sergeant Branch said. "He'll be safer back here at the base of supplies."

Three days later, still in the pouring rain, the Tenth had joined the great procession that was laboring through glutinous red mud in the direction of Stone's River. Cord marched with his drum and haversack, but Tommy and Chris rode high on a supply wagon. Every crossroad was a tangled, lashing jam of men and wagons, each loath to yield precedence in passing. Chris added his yelping clamor to the din until Cord, in desperation, muzzled him with a gun strap, then loosened the ropes on his drum and put Chris inside it.

A halt was made that night twelve miles from Stone's River. It was cold and raw, with deep fog everywhere through which campfires shone weirdly. Another day of marching in the rain brought the Tenth within five miles of Murfreesboro where, to their great disappointment, they were halted and held in reserve. They bivouacked in a clearing while other regiments pressed on past them to man the battle front which, they were told, zigzagged over hills, through woods, and along the sinuous and swampy course of Stone's River some three miles ahead. Far into the night they could hear men and guns still moving forward. Then, just at dawn of the last day of the year, came the sound of heavy firing which began the battle of Stone's River.

Back in the reserve camp as the hours passed and the thunder of the guns grew more menacing, men huddled about reluctant fires, both dreading and desiring the summons forward which might come to them out of the fog at any moment. Toward noon, there was a well-founded rumor that the enemy was pressing hard and reinforcements would be needed to carry the day. Then there were orders for the Tenth to proceed upon a guard march, conducting ammunition by a roundabout road to the advancing left wing of the army. But to Cord, as the regiment was getting under way, came Colonel Lum with another commission.

"Foote, I understand you know your way about these woods pretty well."

"Yes, sir. I do, sir." Cord was breathless with eagerness.

"We can't be responsible for Sergeant Branch's boy in what's coming. I want you to take him to the stockade where his father is stationed. Here's a map will help you." Colonel Lum explained the penciled diagram he had drawn for Cord's direction. "Can you start right away?"

Cord swallowed hard to down the disappointment that nearly choked him. Longing to see and be a part of a real battle, he must turn his back upon it—the steadily increasing roll of the big guns at the front and all the stirring confusion of behind the lines—for the lonely quiet of the forest ways he knew so well. What was it Old Lacey had said, and not too long ago? "I tell you fellows this is *war,* and we've got to stay by and do as we're told."

Cord brought his hand up in perfunctory salute. "Yes, sir."

He called to Chris, knowing the dog would be safer with him and that he would be company on the way back, then he called to Tommy, and they started off.

The two boys kept to the Nashville Turnpike as long as they could, though the railroad track would have been the shorter way. Cord wanted to see the hurrying reinforcements that crowded the road, even though they were constantly being pushed out of the way by them. Standing still for a last look before leaving the turnpike, a regiment came by which proved to be the Illinois 68th. In the midst of it was Jimmie Tyson, pink-cheeked with excitement, astride a big sorrel which was one of a team hitched to the gun limber he was urging forward as fast as possible. His face was wreathed with smiles as he spied the two boys and the dog by the roadside.

"Hi, Sissie!" the boys called to him.

"Hi, boys, we're going to fight! We're goin' to fight 'em to a finish! Just watch the 68th Illinois do for the Johnnies!"

His eager young treble was lost in the clamor of the turnpike. Cord gaped after him with envy in his heart.

The boys plunged into the silence of the dripping-wet woods, through which they trudged until darkness overtook them, and Cord decided to camp for the night. It was a cold, clear night. They built a fire within a sheltering circle of cedars near a spring and had bacon and coffee with their hardtack before they curled up in their blankets to sleep.

"If you want to be warm all night," Cord said knowledgeably, "sleep on the lee side of the fire."

"Why?" Tommy asked.

"Because the fire dries the ground and the heat acts like a blanket. Never mind the smoke. Wouldn't you rather be a baked ham in the morning than a chilled cucumber?"

The distant booming of the guns sounded all through the night. Cord would have felt unbearably lonely were it not for Chris snuggling inside his blanket, and the assurance that he was doing his duty.

They reached the stockade at noon the next day, cold and hungry. But Cord could not be persuaded to stay for more than a bite to eat. He had not been able to hear the guns so far back of the lines and what he was really hungry for was news of the battle. He struck off down the railroad track as the shortest route back, hoping it would bring him near the left wing of the line of battle toward which his regiment had been starting when he left them. It was a longer way than he had thought. That night he and Chris camped again in the forest. No sound of firing could be heard and Cord was consumed with anxiety over what he should find on his return.

The three days away had been days of bitter, obstinate fighting, with forty thousand men engaged on each side.

Cord's wildest imaginings could not have pictured the horrors he saw as he retraced his way, searching for his regiment, over roads that were cruelly rutted at night, a sucking mire at noon. He was miserably aware that a welter of broken and exhausted men were lying about; while other men, farther out, were still being driven back and forth over hills and through woods which were racked and torn by their struggles. Scores and hundreds of the wounded and mangled, many of them dead or dying, were spread upon the ground for want of a better place to lay them, while surgeons worked up to their elbows in blood, and stretcher-bearers constantly brought in more groaning or shrieking victims.

"Who won?" Cord asked, whenever he found anyone who could stop what he was doing long enough to hear a question.

No one could tell him.

"We ain't beat yet," was the only answer he ever got, and that was from a stretcher-bearer.

There were intervals of ominous stillness at the front, but now and again the ground trembled beneath Cord's feet with the roar of the cannon as the battle raged anew at one point or another. It reached its terrible climax in the late afternoon when fifty-eight big guns of the Union batteries west of the river thundered in chorus, raking the enemy lines with their fire in a final repulse. After that there was no more firing.

But still no one seemed certain of the outcome, and all night long there was the sound of men and guns moving over the difficult ground, massing for attack east of the river in the morning. When day came, however, all was quiet with both armies too exhausted for action. At midnight word came that the enemy was retreating.

Cord saw no one he knew or recognized in all the melee until the day after the retreat began, when he came upon the Illinois 68th just withdrawn from the field. They were flung about on the ground like dead men, their horses standing among them with drooping heads. He searched about for Jimmie Tyson, and presently found him sitting on the ground, braced against a gun limber, with his horses standing above him. He was white and drawn, his blue eyes staring wide, glazed and expressionless. Cord gaped a moment, hardly recognizing him.

"Hello, Jimmie," he ventured at last. "You're a fine sight for a conquering hero! What you been doing?"

The boy only stared at him as if he did not hear.

Then a big artilleryman lunged up threateningly and answered for Jimmie.

"What's he been doin' with himself? You impudent mick, I'd like to thrash you! He's been asettin' on a horse for thirty-six hours, night and day—settin' on a horse behind them guns, while the Johnnies charged 'em. Three horses shot out from under him, an' he'd just get another, an' climb on, an' set there like a statue. The rest of us could fight, an' run around an' do something. But that lad's job was just to set there an' keep his horses ready to move the guns any minute. Lord a'mighty, boy, I hope you never know what that means!"

Jimmie seemed to know what he was saying, for he smiled faintly and tried to speak. Cord bent close to hear. "I stuck, Footey. I'm just fagged, that's all."

Someone came along then who told Cord his regiment was a mile or so down the road. Cord didn't know quite what to say to Jimmie, who seemed suddenly far away and a hero.

"Gosh, Jimmie, you're great," he said shyly.

He started off down the road, Chris trotting along beside him, eager to find the boys he had not seen for nearly five days and little thinking that he would never see Jimmie Tyson again.

Around their campfires that night the men pieced together the ebb and flow of the battle at Stone's River. At dawn of the first day, General Bragg had struck boldly and with superb direction at the weakest point in the Union lines. General Rosecrans, conducting his own assault at the opposite end of the three-mile front, had pushed the advance and then rushed back to re-form the lines Bragg's initiative had broken. The Union forces fell back before the onrushing tide of the enemy until General Sheridan's division was reached. Sheridan ordered the countercharge with bayonets fixed, and then stood firm against three massed attacks until all his commanders and nearly two thousand men had been killed. Cartridge boxes empty, he had charged with cold steel and then withdrawn in order to the field where a new battle line was forming.

"Here we are!" he cried, as he met General Rosecrans galloping up. "Here we are—what's left of us!"

His heroic stand saved the day.

But the crisis had not yet passed. The enemy continued to surge forward on both sides until it met with the rocklike resistance of General Thomas's division. Meanwhile a new battle line had formed. Twelve thousand reinforcements rushed to the field. General Rosecrans skillfully massed his artillery on a knoll above the river where it proved impregnable to repeated assaults. The enemy charged four times with magnificent courage, only to retire baffled and torn. The battle surged to another point of attack at the Round Forest where General Rosecrans himself was grazed by a cannon ball that carried away the head of Colonel Garesche, his chief of staff, who was riding at his side. Dauntlessly making his way to the front, Old Rosy ordered a bayonet charge which broke the enemy line and ended the battle in that quarter.

Cord listened to it all, reliving the days of courageous assault and heroic resistance almost as if he had been with his regiment during them. Chris whimpered and Cord reached down to stroke him. "Never mind," he whispered to the little dog, "we'll be in a battle someday."

CHAPTER V

CORD WAS DESOLATE. Somewhere in the ninety-mile confusion of the march of the Michigan Tenth back to Nashville, he had lost Chris. No one had seen the little black dog; no one had heard his shrill familiar bark; but there was not a man who did not promise to keep a sharp lookout for him.

Nashville had been turned into a military hospital and the members of the Drum Corps reported to the Sanitary Commission for their orders. Some were immediately detailed as stretcher-bearers; Cord, small and quickfooted, was dispatched as water carrier. Public buildings and private dwellings were filled with wounded from both armies. And still they came—in creaking, high-wheeled ambulances, jolting supply wagons, rickety farm carts from which they were carried into hastily set up army tents until better shelter could be devised or requisitioned. Cord forgot his own misery in the torn white agony of the men among whom he moved. Their moans and delirious murmurings, as well as their courage, plucky smiles and banter, made him want to do anything he could to help them.

One of the first to whom he gave water was a Johnny Reb with both arms injured. Cord had to lift him before he could drink, lift him ever so gently but awkwardly because he didn't know in the least how to do it. He braced the injured man sturdily while he drank from the canteen held to his lips. When it was emptied, the man sank back with a groan. After a moment he opened his eyes and the shadow of a smile crossed his face as he looked at the solemn-eyed boy who was watching him so anxiously. Cord bent down to refill the canteen from a pail of water.

"Did I clean you out, little Yank?"

"That's all right, Johnny Reb," Cord answered, smiling back.

"Time was, little Yank, when I'da ducked you good an' propah if you'd come nigh me with that pail o' watah. But right now, I'm mighty glad to put it inside o' me. Thank you, little Yank, that tasted good."

"You're welcome, Johnny Reb."

The soldier closed his eyes with a sigh of satisfaction.

Cord shouldered his string of canteens and trudged on with his pail of water. That afternoon he took pains to return to his Johnny Reb, only to find another man in his place.

"Never opened his eyes again," the soldier on the next cot said. "Just plain bled to death, I guess, poor devil."

Cord found his way back to his tent that night, tired beyond any tiredness he had known before, and lonely for the feel of that little black squirming body in his arms and the warm tongue licking all over his face.

"Go to bed, boy," Old Lacey said. "The Drum Corps can sound taps for once without you."

Cord shook his head. He wasn't sleepy and he couldn't

bear to lie down. He felt as if he'd never get up again if he did. So many of the men he had seen that day would not get up again.

"I'm all right, Pop."

Old Lacey put his hand on Cord's shoulder for a moment, then he went out of the tent. Cord thought of writing home and collected pen and paper, but with these spread out on the upturned box before him he went no further. There was nothing he wanted to tell them back home. For a long time he sat hunched over in dejection, chin in hand, gravely watching the sputtering flame of the candle as it burned lower. After a while he found himself writing, not a letter but something resembling a poem—

> Home I have left, and what is it for,
> To lead a life of civil war,
> To be deprived of all that's dear,
> To lead a life of dread and fear.
>
> It was for my sweet Country's sake
> That I such sacrifice did make.
> I left my home and friends behind
> Far different circles for to find.
>
> I took up arms against the foe,
> I gave to them the deadly blow,
> That our sweet Country might be once more
> As it was in the days of yore.
>
> So far I have spent my time in vain,
> At least, I think we have nothing gained.

He knew that he had not said much, but it made him feel better to have put down what he did. Soon it would be time for tattoo, then taps. Cord took his drum down from its hook and put the belt over his shoulder. With a finger he tested the sound that came from the batter head. The cold damp weather was hard on drums. He released the snares to improve the tone, then tried it again. The tension had to be right to give the maximum tone to a roll and Cord felt that though he could not write much in the way of poetry, he could get his drum to perform as it should. When Old Lacey's call came, he was ready to go out into the night and do his duty as drummer boy of Company F.

He slept well that night. He was wakened early by a face washing given him by a warm pink tongue. He sat up to make sure he wasn't dreaming. Chris looked at him. The next moment his shrill bark would have wakened the other drummers in the tent. Cord caught him in his arms and pulled him under the blanket. There was no need to wake the regiment, Cord whispered to him, ready to forgive Chris his wanderings because he had come back again.

Night after night around the campfires that scented the winter dark, men relived the battle of Stone's River as further reports of it came in. Stubbornly fought and victorious as it had been, the Army of the Cumberland realized that the small gain resulting from it was far from commensurate with the frightful human loss. Thirteen thousand men had been killed or injured on the Union side and at least ten thousand on the Confederate. This terrible sacrifice had purchased only the withdrawal of the Confederates from Murfreesboro to Shelbyville, thirty miles distant, and a corresponding advance of the Federals, whose base of supplies was now moved southward thirty miles from Nashville to Murfreesboro.

Within a week, the division to which the Tenth belonged was ordered to remove camp to a new base of supplies; but the Tenth was retained as garrison at Nashville with headquarters still at Cherry Creek. The men had time to repair their equipment, to rest up before the next march wherever it might lead, and to write letters home. Writing was never an easy labor to Cord, but he knew that his letters meant a great deal to his mother and father. Between battles and marches, he did his best to keep them abreast of his doings.

                                                      Nashvill Tenn
                                                    Jany 28th 1863

Dear Parents
haveing answered
a letter that I received from George
and now take the oppertunity to answer your kind letter which I received last night and the night before last I received one from George Turner and have answerd. the ninth Michigan is at Murfreesboro. I did not find out in time to see Del Parcelo. I am selling news papers for an old man he pays me good for it I have go in the other regiments and sell them for him. there is two or three of the boys writing by one candle and I cannot hardley see. I spoke to Gill Alport about the box and he said that he would fetch me the box when it come. the letter that I got from George is dated the 17th and he said he had received the letter that I wrote to him and he said the had their things all done up and ready to march. our Ajutant was hurt yesterday by his horse falling on him. I wrote a long letter to you and one to Mr. Bennetts folks and one to Hannah and I think that I have done my share of writing for a while you must give my kindest regards to them that sent me them things. I would write but if I should it would get a corrispondance and if I should get up a one I am afraid that I should not be able to keep it up you must not think that I mean Mr. Bennetts folks for I do not nor none of them that I have been in the habbit of Corrissponding you must therefore give my kindest regards to them and tell them if you see fit the reason why is because I cannot write to them all. one of our boys has just come up from down town drunk as he can be. I have not had any letter from Hannah yet and I cannot think why she does not write to me. I will earn enough to pay my debts and then I can send more home I will send you all that I can. my

company is on Picketit tonight I am glad that I do not have to stand Picket for they will suffer tonight for it is cold enough to freeze a man we have to keep our Over Coats on to keep warm and in the tent to. the weather is cold now as we have had since I cam down south. there was a fire in the town today it did not amount to much. I was down to it. there was one engine there they have got Steam Engines here they are nice I tell you. I cannot think of much more. I think that your dress is very nice and if youwant you may use some of my money. your dress is just as pretty as it can be and I am glad sent it to me. I have made up my mind not to buy the drum for a penney saved is a penney earned and I can send it home. tell Alley that I am just as much Obliged as if he had sent me the papers and stamps tell him I am gointo write to hime and he must write to me I have writin to him and have not had any answer from it there is a good many woulded in the town and they are shipping them as fast as they can I sent your paper last night and I am gointo send you a piece of poertrey in this letter I guess that I will not write anything more to night and finish it tomorrow. haveing sold all my papers I now take the oppitunity to finish my letter. I had an accident while I was peddeling my papers there is a dog where I go sell my papers and I had just been in the tend and was just comeing out when the dog bite me it was a pretty good bite. I put some tobbaco on it and it feels better I guess that it will get well I cannot think of anything more this time goodbye from your affectionate son

CORIDON . E . FOOTE

Day after day, all during late winter and early spring, the Michigan Tenth as guardians of the cracker line marched with the wagon trains, did picket duty, made repairs to the railroad, loaded and unloaded supplies. The men would have grumbled less had they been in the front-line fighting, and their officers had constantly to remind them that there would be no battle line without a cracker line.

Vast quantities of food and equipment, far more than could be conveyed by the railroad alone, had to be moved to Murfreesboro. The Tenth, doing guard duty with the wagon trains, accompanied as many as six hundred wagons at a time. The drummers marched before their companies, giving the signals and setting the tempo, but marching often had to be slowed to the weary pace of the six-mule-team wagons that jolted over the rutted roads still clogged with the aftermath of battle—haversacks, blankets and broken muskets, tent poles, overturned wagons spilling their loads of oats or flour or medical supplies made useless by the weather and the trampling of animal hoofs and soldiers' feet.

Conscious of what they could do to help men lift their feet out of the mire and even get the mules to hauling, the members of the Drum Corps did their untiring best. Five miles was not too long to drum at a stretch, ceasing whenever the soldiers approached a bridge so their step would be broken when crossing it. But rarely did any one of them drum for so much as a mile without having to lend a hand to right an upset wagon or help push one through the mud. In crisp weather the drummers could produce snappy tones that pleased them; in damp weather they did what they could to offset flabby tones. But whatever the weather, Cord and Ira Miles now drummed as they had never drummed before. Each one had become the possessor of a handsome new silver-mounted drum, Christmas gifts from their companies which had come through tardily from Boston, delayed by the concentration of food and ammunition preceding the battle of Stone's River.

Ira played from years of experience. Cord, gaining in skill, held his new drum in great respect. He knew now that he would not struggle with its ropes to unloose the head and to put contraband inside. The silver-mounted drum was not to be used as an extra haversack; it was something to care for and handle with pride. Perhaps he would even wear it back to Flint at the end of the war, drumming the Michigan Tenth home as he had drummed them away.

Camping one night near the little settlement of Lavergne, the men woke the next morning to find themselves surrounded by thick fog. They had hardly got under way with the wagon train when a great shouting and firing in the rear brought them to uncertain halt as officers rode back to investigate. The sound of fighting continued to come to them out of the fog for perhaps ten minutes, then it was followed by a receding clatter of horses' hoofs. The order came to resume their lumbering pace forward. Presently two mounted officers came abreast them, leading a string of the most nondescript men Cord had ever seen. Tattered, unkempt, bristling with scorn for their captors, they were slinking and furtive as well, more like animals than men.

"Guerrillas!"

The word passed along the train in a kind of sibilant snarl as the marching men shouted curses and taunts at the prisoners. It was their first encounter with these outlaw marauders who preyed upon both sides, and were hated alike by North and South as perpetrators of some of the most cruel outrages of the time. There were fifteen of them in the captive string, and as many more had been killed or wounded by the picketing Companies A and D at the rear. The guerrillas marched sullenly under heavy guard, midway of the slow-moving wagon train.

By late afternoon, the Tenth reached the straggling town of Murfreesboro. Shortly beyond where the Nashville Turnpike crossed Stone's River, the unloading began. A branch road angled back toward the railroad, and here several trainloads of supplies had already been piled in great teetering caches, each one larger than a country schoolhouse. There were hundreds of slabs of bacon, corded in tall rectangles, boxes of hardtack, burlap bags of navy beans, canvas bags of coffee beans, and crates upon crates of five-gallon cans of desiccated vegetables. These were the newest item of the commissariat and consisted of carrots, beets and cabbage which had been placed while still green under enormous pressure until all the moisture was removed, and the dry residue was then sealed up in huge tin cans. From this a queer tasteless soup was made, designed to prevent scurvy, which had become prevalent with the bacon and hardtack diet of recent months.

The men of the cracker line realized that such vast stores of food represented a very real triumph in railway guarding and reconstruction. There were thirty miles or more of slender steel railway to be kept intact, railway that went through mountainous wilds infested with guerrillas and patrolled by enemy cavalry. Upon that precarious route between Louisville and Nashville, Nashville and Murfreesboro, seventy thousand men and their animals were almost wholly dependent for subsistence. The enemy worked constantly to destroy the line—burning stations and cars, demolishing engines, choking tunnels with rubbish; and there was not a bridge or trestle of consequence that had not been destroyed and rebuilt, some of them many times.

Sergeant Branch with fifteen men had been detailed to guard a trestle in a wild ravine just south of Lavergne. Cord found his way to their lonely stockade frequently. He was always welcome. Big Tom was glad to have a companion for his small son, and as soon as Cord appeared the two boys would head for the rugged woodland with its dense cedar brakes and steep mountain trails.

One cold and foggy morning the boys had gone out to look for game. Attracted by a construction and repair train, three cars long, steaming slowly down the track from the direction of Nashville, the boys raced behind it and hooked a ride. The train stopped at a nearby crossroad, pickets were posted, and the construction crew set to work bolting rails more securely where the ties appeared to have been tampered with. The job was soon done and the boys persuaded the guards to let them ride farther down the line. The engineer signaled for the pickets to return.

Suddenly the sound of firing came from along the road where pickets had been posted. In another moment two pickets came out of the fog crying the alarm as they ran toward the train, turning back to fire up the road as they ran. With a thunder of horses' hoofs and that bloodcurdling fox hunters' cry which Cord had learned was the Rebel yell, a troop of enemy cavalry in full regalia dashed in upon them, completely surrounding them, intercepting the pickets on either side. The Rebs dismounted and swarmed over the train while their horses milled about in snorting and stamping confusion.

There were all of two hundred in the attacking party, but to Cord they seemed as little to be measured in numbers as the gray fog out of which they came. The guards resisted pluckily, shooting from the shelter of their cars; but they were soon overpowered as the enemy swarmed up over the tops of the cars, seized the guards from above, and carried them off as prisoners. Then they set fire to the train.

In the confusion, the two boys escaped into the woods and were off on the run toward the stockade manned by Sergeant Tom. Before they had gone halfway, they met the sergeant and his fifteen men coming up at a stealthy doublequick and heading for the sound of the shooting. The boys turned back with them to the scene of the attack. The shooting had ceased. Taking cover in a cedar brake, they watched the Johnnie Rebs distributing their prisoners and collecting their wounded, while flames crackled along the length of two of the cars.

"Now, listen, men," Sergeant Tom gave hoarsely whispered instructions, "there's a holy mob of Johnnies out there. They can blink us in a minute if they find out how few we are. Come along now, every man o' ye, and let's out an' at 'em yelling bloody murder, and shooting as hard an' straight as we can. They won't know what's struck 'em. They'll think it's hell let loose—an' so it is. Come on, men!"

He charged out at the head of his men, yelling louder than all the rest.

The counterattack was a complete surprise. Mounted men spurred their horses and were down the road at a gallop, despite the efforts of an officer to rally them, and riderless horses went plunging after them. Most of the prisoners were recovered by Sergeant Tom, and six Rebels were captured besides the several wounded that were left by the rout; also ten horses and considerable arms. There followed a time of desperate chopping of wood and beating out of flames in which Cord and small Tommy joined, with the result that one car was saved in fairly good condition. The prisoners and wounded were put into it, and the battered train went steaming on to Murfreesboro.

Sergeant Tom and his men led off the captured horses to the stockade. The boys followed, giving a hand wherever they could.

Winter melted into spring. The Tenth stayed on at the Cherry Creek camp, and nothing particular happened. Cord learned to know Nashville like his own home town, as well as much of the countryside. With Chris, he followed Cherry Creek to the Cumberland, returning with rabbits and squirrels which he gave to Wardie for a stew. At night Cord and Chris went ratting. Sometimes a rowdy gang of soldiers hung about and made bets on their prowess; but more often they hunted alone, long after taps. In the cold moonlight Cord would sit by the hour, motionless over a rathole in a dirty runway. Chris sat between his knees, held firmly by the collar made from the worn-out gun strap, until an unwary rat poked its head out. With a throaty snarl the terrier was upon it. Chris's quick sureness and the savage gusto with which he finished off his capture were gratifying to Cord. This was war, too.

Cord's pie business still flourished, though flour was running low; and he also earned something extra by selling newspapers. He read them carefully too, hoping to find out why nothing happened and why, why, why they just stood at Nashville. It seemed that the whole country was wondering much the same thing. Cord read of General Halleck's dramatic offer of the rank of major general in the regular army to the commander who would soonest win an important victory. General Grant had ignored the letter, the papers said, but General Rosecrans treated it as an insult. He replied to Halleck that he "felt degraded at such auctioning of honors." If there was a general, Rosecrans said, who would fight for his own personal preferment when he would not for the sake of his country, he should be despised by all honorable men.

"Three cheers for Old Rosy!" The men of the Army of the Cumberland applauded the high spirits of their commander. But they did wish something would happen.

One April day a regimental detail of forty-six men from the Tenth, in command of Lieutenant Vanderburgh, was sent with an ammunition train to Murfreesboro. Cord persuaded the lieutenant to let him ride down with them as far as Sergeant Tom's stockade. He rode the engine with Lieutenant Vanderburgh and the engineer, enjoying his springtime excursion to the full and wishing he need not leave the train as it neared its destination. Then a low exclamation from the engineer told them that all was not well.

His quick eye had detected a slightly misplaced rail just ahead, and his hand found the brake as he uttered a warning. If they had not been running slowly the whole train would have been thrown from the track; as it was, the engine came to a halt with a grinding of wheels and hissing of steam. Two of the cars behind it overturned, dragging the engine off the track. The engineer and the riders jumped free just as a horde of guerrillas burst upon them from the cedar brake at the right of the track.

Several of the men escaping from the train were wounded by gunfire. Lieutenant Vanderburgh was shot in the foot, but sprang up quickly. Calling to his men to fortify themselves behind the cars and never say die, he scrambled over the train. With rapid revolver fire he led the resistance to the attack. Wounded again, and outnumbered, Lieutenant Vanderburgh led his men back from the track a short distance to refuge behind a cedar fence built around two small houses and a garden patch. Some of the guerrillas pursued them, while others swarmed over the train looking for plunder.

Cord, escaping from the train, had taken cover in some bushes near the track. When he saw the lieutenant fall again and not get up as he had twice before, Cord was galvanized into action. Lieutenant Nicholls, taking command, led the men in retreat beyond the two houses into the forest. Cord set off on the run to Sergeant Tom's stockade. He raced ahead through the woods, sped by the fury that filled him against the marauders who had shot down Lieutenant Vanderburgh. Sergeant Tom and his men, in search of the firing, were approaching at the double-quick, and Cord was relieved to meet them.

"What's going on down there, Footey?" was the sergeant's low-voiced greeting.

"It's guerrillas, sir," Cord told him breathlessly, "a howling mob of 'em! They've wrecked the train and killed old Vandie—"

"Are you all that got away?"

"No, sir. There's some comin' back with Lieutenant Nicholls. You'll find 'em in a minute, if you keep on. Oh, sir, can't you make 'em go back an' scare off those devil guerrillas the way you did the Johnnies a while ago?"

There was a responsive gleam in Sergeant Tom's eyes. "Sure I can, boy, as sure as my name's Big Tom." He turned to give instructions to one of his men to go back to the stockade and send the other five men, while he went on to the scene of the attack.

Soon the remnants of those who had escaped from the train led by Lieutenant Nicholls were joined by Sergeant Tom and his men. They made their low-voiced plans, scarcely a stone's throw from the blazing train, while they waited for reinforcements from the stockade. Cord stayed close to the big Irishman, ready to carry out any order he might be given.

Lieutenant Nicholls and Sergeant Branch decided to separate their forces. Taking advantage of the cover given by the burgeoning foliage, they thought to close in from two sides. The unwary guerrillas, still moving about the flaming train, sorting out plunder and gathering their wounded for departure, would be taken by surprise.

When Sergeant Tom and his men burst upon them with a mighty yelling and firing, and Lieutenant Nicholls and his men appeared no less savagely from another quarter, the guerrillas were routed by the suddenness and violence of the attack. Springing to horse, almost without offering any resistance, they fled wildly along the track and into the woods, leaving their plunder, eight riderless horses, and six dead upon the field.

It was too late to save the burning cars, but the ammunition stores had been removed from them by the attackers and lay piled not far away. The engine was laboriously put upon the track and presently thrashed away backwards toward Nashville, with the mortally wounded Lieutenant Vanderburgh aboard and a man to take care of him. Cord never saw him again.

For several hours the men of the two details worked to clear the wreckage from the tracks. They carried the wounded to the nearby houses where they were made as comfortable as possible. The ammunition that had been salvaged was stored inside the cedar fence until a later train could pick it up. At sundown, twenty men of the forty-six who had set out that morning returned to the Cherry Creek camp, led by Cord through the woods by a short cut which he knew. Twenty-one of the forty-six had been sacrificed to guarding the cracker line; the rest lay wounded.

Sergeant Tom received a letter of commendation from General Rosecrans, as well as a promotion. Now he was Lieutenant Tom and his office was that of divisional wagon master.

As the Army of the Cumberland spread its lines through the region of Murfreesboro, it gradually covered a front fifty miles in extent. The cracker line of the railway had to be supplemented by ever-lengthening wagon trains which wound their way by mule team over narrow, mountainous roads and enemy-beset forest paths. The complex business of their oversight became Big Tom's charge. He rose to the demands of his new position and to its privileges as well. He was given a horse, a tent, and a servant of his own, and a little gray donkey for Tommy to ride.

Lieutenant Tom was a heroic figure as he commanded a crossroads where two wagon trains converged, sitting his prancing black horse and cracking his long, snakelike whip to emphasize orders. Cord and Tommy would often go miles, taking turns at riding the donkey, to watch Lieutenant Tom. He had his own way of placating the sullen drivers when they were forced to give way. For them it usually meant a long hour's sitting behind switching-tailed mules while the other train plodded across their front, sometimes with leering grins and occasionally insolent remarks.

"Now don't be gettin' so pert about your good fortune there, me man," Lieutenant Tom would call out to a braggart driver. "It's not for any good ye ever did that I'm givin' ye the right o' way! Sure, an' it's only because ye've got twice as far to drive those blitherin' beasts that ye can't get above a crawl. Git along, now! Eyes front! An' wipe off that silly grin!"

He could take a different tone with another driver. "Never bother yourselves, men! Ye'll be paradin' acrost their front the next time. Give 'em their day. Ye'll have yours, my lads! Take it easy. Take it easy now."

And again he might say, "Sure, an' you men need a little rest," as he rode down the line that came to a grudging halt. "Your beasts look all tuckered out. Just snatch a wink while ye kin, boys, an' thank the good Lord for the chancet! Snatch a wink, an' make up for that late game o' yours last night!"

The great event was the encounter with the train of another wagon master, for then Lieutenant Tom had to parley with one of his own kind; but he was known as a fair man, and unless there was special reason for precedence the practice was simple: The train whose front wagons arrived first had right of way. The approach to crossroads was often a wild race, with wagon masters galloping up and down the roadside urging their drivers to the utmost effort, and with drivers lashing and swearing and shouting at their mules, since a moment's lateness might hold them up for half a day.

It was also the task of the wagon master to see that his drivers kept close together, for the muleteers of the waiting train were ever ready to lash their beasts forward and cut through the first possible gap in his lumbering ranks, when his train must stop and, in turn, watch its chance to break through.

"Larrup along there, men!" Lieutenant Branch would shout as he galloped beside them flourishing his rawhide whip. "There's room for a house and lot between yez. Nuzzle up, I tells ye! Step lively, an' don't leave nose room for them blasted beasts awaitin' up the road there! Larrup along, I tells ye, larrup along!"

One May morning Cord set out from Nashville with a wagon train. He was the proud possessor of twenty-four hours' leave, and with Chris beside him he was going to make the most of it. Sometimes he rode on one of the wagons, often he trudged along beside the train looking for nests in the trees and bushes that grew by the roadside. When he found a clutch of eggs, he would remove one carefully and put it in his haversack. He wanted to add unusual ones to his collection at home, though he wondered constantly how he could ever get them back to Flint. The day was mild, the countryside lush with new foliage, and Cord would have been content to ride on endlessly with the wagon train. By starlight, they crossed Stone's River and presently ambled in to the base of supplies at Murfreesboro.

Cord hunted about until he found Tommy and his father camped near the corrals. While their man Jim prepared supper, the boys had a swim in the creek running near. Jim said he had everything for a feast except some eggs, but that there didn't appear to be a laying hen left in all the countryside.

"Eggs!" Cord exclaimed. "My haversack is full o' eggs. I

was for sending them home, but you can have them if you want them."

He laid his haversack on the ground and took out the eggs that he had wrapped carefully in grass and leaves. "You can tell most of 'em—the blue egg is catbird and the biggest one is blue jay and the white one is pigeon. The smallest one I don't know. That one that has so many and such large spots on it is mockingbird. You can't find their eggs in Michigan."

Jim's eyes were snapping at the sight of so many eggs, small though they were, and he grinned with pleasure. "Now, it's a real feast that I'll be givin' ye, indeed it is!"

And feast it was—fresh bacon and fried eggs, new bread and apple pie which Jim had procured from a nearby farmhouse, and coffee.

Later, Big Tom lay on the grass smoking his pipe. The boys sat close to the dwindling fire, talking about the campaign that was being planned for the summer.

"Aye, but I'll be sendin' Tommy home before then," Big Tom said.

Cord looked startled, surprised that anyone would want to leave the war; then he saw a chance of getting some of his treasures home.

"I've got a nice little cavalry cartridge box that I could pack my eggs in, and a cavalry belt you could wear," Cord began, "and some more things. I'd like it, Tommy, if you could get them back to Flint for me."

Tommy's serious face brightened. "War's not what I thought it would be," he said.

"War!" Cord exclaimed. "You haven't been in a battle yet."

Then Tommy winked slyly. "And maybe I'll not be goin' at all, at all," he said.

Soon Big Tom announced bedtime and the boys went off to Lieutenant Branch's tent.

In the morning, there was all the excitement and stir of

getting the wagon train started back to Nashville. Cord was standing near Big Tom and Tommy, waiting his chance for a ride for himself and Chris, when General Rosecrans rode up with two of his staff.

"Good work, Lieutenant," the boys heard him say to Big Tom, but for all their listening they could neither catch nor make sense of the general's ensuing words.

Lieutenant Branch beamed with pleasure as he saluted and watched the general ride away, then he looked at the two boys.

"An' did ye hear what the general sez to me, boys? Ye young rapscallions that don't think yez are in the army without yez are shootin' up Johnnies at the front! The general sez to me, sez he, there couldn't be no front without a back, an' he sez to me, an army can't live without its stomick. Me, here"—he waved his arm in a sweeping gesture that included the acres of wagons—"me, here, boys, I'll have yez know—I'm the stomick!"

CHAPTER VI

IN JUNE, the Tenth was ordered to Murfreesboro. The men knew that Chattanooga was their objective, two hundred miles farther south. If it was attained, it would sever the main arteries of the Confederacy. Rumors of a great advance ran through the regiment. Newspapers that reached the men, including the weekly that Cord received from his parents, as well as the news that traveled within the ranks, had long told stories of the loyalty to the Union of the helplessly isolated people of Chattanooga.

The Drum Corps beat General Assembly and the soldiers formed by companies, then with colors flying and the drummers marching at the head of their companies the men swung along at their best gait, leaving the Cherry Creek camp behind and heading into the rich green country of Tennessee. The wagons followed.

"We're going in the right direction, boys," Old Lacey said, proud of his drummers who set the pace and kept the regiment marching.

When the Army of the Cumberland began its advance on the 24th of June, the Tenth Michigan and the Sixtieth Illinois were left behind as garrison at Murfreesboro. Bulletins of the advancing army stirred envious interest as the Cumberland divisions swept steadily forward. The enemy fell back before them from Shelbyville and Tullahoma, unresisting, to fortify themselves in the mountain fastnesses of Chattanooga. When word reached the Tenth that General Rosecrans had established the new base of supplies at Stevenson, Alabama, men from all over the regiment rushed to find the spot on Pop Lacey's map. Hard upon these bulletins of progress came the good news from the West that Vicksburg had fallen, and from the East, terrible as the cost had been, of the victory at Gettysburg. It began to look as if the Stars and Stripes might someday wave again over a united country.

The men of the Tenth, disappointed though they were that they were not yet in the fighting, celebrated the Fourth of July with songs and cheers for Generals Grant and Meade and Rosecrans and the gallant men they led, as they sat around their campfires and waited for orders to advance and join the victorious armies.

"We'll be home before another winter sets in," Old Lacey said.

A few of the older men echoed the word "home" as if they dared to let themselves think of something that could again be real; but the younger men looked at each other anxiously.

"Who wants to go home before we've fought a battle?" George Jay asked.

Cord nodded. Fond of Pop Lacey as he was, it was George who spoke for him then.

Following the triple flare of achievement, action everywhere seemed to cease. At least, so it appeared to the men of the Tenth as they lay baking in Murfreesboro through the hot, dust-choked weeks of July and August. News was scarce. Their mail had gone astray with the advance. The world seemed standing still, and they were like men forgotten. A few months ago winter cold had been their enemy; now it was summer heat and boredom, insect pests and diminishing rations.

The bacon, corded in huge piles which were exposed to dust and flies and weather, became infested with maggots. It could be eaten only after soaking each ration in a camp kettle full of water until the maggots came floating to the top to be poured off with the water. Besides this stale and soggy bit of meat which was their mainstay, the daily ration was four pieces of hardtack and a teaspoonful each of coffee beans and sugar. Now and then there was a bowl of watery soup made from desiccated vegetables. Sometimes, on a day's march, there was a chance to lay hold of an unsuspecting chicken and bring it back for a company to roast over its campfire. Often, when passing a springhouse of a farm, men would break ranks, rush in, and drink all the milk they found cooling in pails. It was not difficult for men to feel they had a right to whatever food they could lay their hands on in a hostile countryside, and their officers could do little to restrain them. Even a potato field tempted men. Swarming over it, they tore potatoes out of the ground and ate them raw and whole with the earth still on them. Benumbed by the slow hunger that was gnawing at them and bored by idleness, scurvy, and dysentery, the regiment suffered a heavy toll of morale from drinking and gambling.

Cord might have been as desperate as the men if it had not been for Chris and his companionship. Old Lacey often shook his head when he watched the two together, knowing what the dog did for the boy; but he knew, too, what might be ahead for them all. Battle was hardly the place for a boy; it was most certainly not the place for a little dog.

"Before we march again, Cordie," he said, "whyn't you find a nice home for Chris and leave him in it?"

Cord protested, but the more he thought about it the more he could understand that Old Lacey was right. He had seen the aftermath of battle. He wouldn't want to see Chris caught up in it.

Late in August orders came to advance, and the drums beat out the call. Men who had been slack and wretched for weeks responded to the stimulus of action. They moved slowly with the wagons in a southwesterly direction as far as Columbia, where they rested for two days. It was there that Cord found a home for Chris, and there that he said good-by. It was almost too much to think that he would see the little black dog again, but Cord told himself that he could hope. There was no regulation in the army that said a man couldn't do that.

Cord gave the leash to the woman who had taken a liking to Chris and who had promised to treat him like her own, then Cord bent over to stroke the shaggy head. "I've got a war to win, Chris, and you—well, you go on catching rats."

"You're a mighty little soldier," the woman said. "Where do you live?"

"In Michigan."

"What state is that in?"

Cord stared at her, then he suddenly turned and ran as fast as he could back to the drummers' tent.

The next morning they marched directly south from Columbia at a faster pace, leaving the wagons to trail behind. Four days' marching brought them sixty miles to Athens, Alabama, where they camped until the wagons caught up with them. Forty miles more at good speed, through increasingly rugged country, and they had reached Huntsville where they stopped again to await the wagons. Another long swing of sixty-five miles at their best pace brought them to Stevenson and reunited them with their division on September 7th. It had been a glorious march—two hundred and twenty-seven miles in twenty days, counting detours through the mountains.

"We could never have done it without the drums," an officer said to Old Lacey.

Pop smiled. "Some may say an army marches on its stomach, but it marches with the drums." The drum major was proud of his men, especially proud of the drummer boy of Company F. It was the first time in months that Cord had marched without a small dog trotting beside him. Old Lacey guessed a little of what had gone into Cord's vigorous drumming on the road from Columbia.

Stevenson was not only the base of supplies but the largest encampment Cord had yet seen. That evening, when word raced through the camp that the enemy had evacuated Chattanooga following General Rosecrans' bombardment in the afternoon, a thundering cheer went up. Later, when the general attended by his staff rode into headquarters, he was greeted by cheer after cheer. Scores of bonfires were lighted. Everywhere there was jubilation. Two Massachusetts regiments swung into camp to the stirring rhythm of the "Battle Hymn of the Republic," and soon the martial strains were echoing from campfire to campfire:

> "Glory! Glory Hallelujah! Glory! Glory Hallelujah!
> Glory! Glory Hallelujah! His truth is marching on.
> He has sounded forth the trumpet that shall never
>   call retreat;
> He is sifting out the hearts of men before His
>   judgment seat:
> Oh, be swift, my soul, to answer Him! be jubilant
>   my feet!

Our God is marching on!
Glory! Glory Hallelujah!"

As the moon swung high above the treetops and the stars paled before it, martial songs gave way to pensive singing:

"Just before the battle, mother, I am thinking most
   of you,
While upon the field we're watching, with the enemy
   in view.
Comrades brave are round me lying, filled with
   thoughts of home and God;
For well they know that on the morrow some will
   sleep beneath the sod.
Farewell, mother, you may never, you may never,
   mother,
Press me to your heart again.
But, oh, you'll not forget me,
Mother, you will not forget me
If I'm numbered with the slain."

Old Lacey began to signal to the Drum Corps, but before they could rise for taps an Irish voice swung into "The Girl I Left Behind Me." One company after another joined in and the four gay, lilting verses were sung; then the drummers sounded taps and stood at attention while the bugles repeated the call. When George Jay and Cord hung up their drums in the drummers' tent, they agreed that at last war was beginning to be rather like what they had imagined it would be.

Their tent was pitched beside the corrals where hundreds of mules and artillery horses had been quartered since June. The night was hot and still. The stench was stifling. Old Lacey sat up in his cot and looked over at the boys. Their eyes were wide open.

"Not asleep?" he asked cautiously.

"Not in that stink," George Jay said.

"Come on then, let's go for a stroll. We can see most anything in this moonlight."

They passed familiar tents, they went by groups of men rolled in their blankets and waiting for sleep, they went around piles of war equipment waiting for use; then they approached a part of the camp where many people were still awake, moving about a huge fire, shuffling and singing. The white light of the moon and the orange glow from the fire shone on their black bodies swaying rhythmically and silently.

"Contraband," Old Lacey whispered, then he told the boys that during the great advance through Tennessee and Alabama, runaway slaves had flocked to the Army of the Cumberland by scores and hundreds. Here, at Stevenson, they were herded into a vast contraband camp.

They were humming together about their fire as if the spirit of jubilation which the soldiers had shared had spilled over to them. The sound they made was strange and melodious, like nothing Cord had ever heard before. Praise was in it, and thanksgiving, yet both seemed to merge with a moaning chorus of lament. As the members of the Drum Corps stood still, watching and listening, the humming of the prisoner slaves swelled in volume until they started singing as if they could no longer contain what was surging up within them. They were led by a big powerful man with the voice of a prophet. His half-naked body showed great jagged scars from the lash of the slave driver; his eyes gleamed with strange ardor in the light of the fire.

"I've heard they call him Jeremiah," Old Lacey said.

Arms outstretched toward the stars, Jeremiah swayed and gesticulated, then slapped his thighs in exultation. When his voice rolled out, it seemed that every word he uttered came from deep within him:

> "Oh, de Lawd He heaped de great sea waves!
> He jes as strong as den!
> He say de word—las' night we slaves,
> Today, de Lawd's free men!
> An' de yam will grow
> An' de cotton blow
> An' we'll have de rice an' de cawn;
> An' don' you fear if never you hear
> De driver blow his hawn!"

Then all the others around the fire—men half-naked, women in loose-fitting linsey-woolsey dresses—lifted their arms and shouted, "Lawd God A'mighty!"

Jeremiah sang out again and this time the people joined in with a moaning entreaty: "Dear, good Lawd!"

The moving, velvety shadows cast by the fire and the moonlight doubled, tripled the group in size.

"Makes you think of Kingdom Come, doesn't it, boys?"

"Sure does, Pop," George Jay whispered hoarsely.

Cord nodded, too awed to speak.

Later, when the drummers went back to their tent, the mournful cadences of the Negro harmonies seemed to have become a part of them. Cord could not have put into words what he was feeling, but he knew now why he was in the war.

Night after night, Cord and George Jay went down to the contraband corral. There were times when the rhythmic intensity of the Negro songs held a sweetness so like pain that Cord found himself swallowing hard, and shivering, and wondering how the Lord God could resist such pleading. There were other times when a happy-go-lucky strain was foremost. Men clapped their hands, one twanged an old banjo, and women danced:

> "Ah wen' down south t' N'Orleans—
> Ah didn' go fer t' stay,

But ah met up wid a yaller gel
An' ah couldn' git away . . ."

During the daytimes it was the animal corrals that interested Cord the most. He made many friends among the muleteers and he was always ready to do whatever he could for them. They responded with valuable favors; one even let Cord try his hand with a six-mule team while everyone else looked on. It was in the mule corral that Cord met some cameramen and before he knew it he and George Jay were posing for their pictures with mules as a background.

The Stevenson camp seemed to the boys as entertaining as a county fair, even after the first rains of autumn had turned the firm trodden hardpan into a gummy waste and brought a hint of winter chill. There was always something to do, and there were the sutlers. Never before had the boys seen more than a few sutlers. At Stevenson they saw hundreds of the itinerant tradesmen who came through the camp with their enticing wares. Their wagons had begun to appear on turnpikes and byroads alike, wherever hungry soldiers might be found to whom they could sell cakes, cookies, nuts and sweets, tobaccos and liquors. The half-starved soldiers welcomed their wares but resented having to pay for them, asking each other why white-livered tradesmen should be making money out of their dire need.

Since May, many of the regiments had received no pay. A soldier could grumble more or less good-naturedly about food and weather; he grumbled bitterly when the Government failed to get his $13 a month to him. Sutlers' supplies began to be looked upon as fair plunder for anyone clever enough to make away with them. The sutlers kept their main stock at Stevenson not far from the commissary stores, piled in great canvas-covered blocks, and guarded night and day by details from the various regiments. The guards managed to be so considerately blind to the nighttime forays of their fellow soldiers that the harassed sutlers were at last compelled to hire a revenue officer to protect their supplies.

Cord knew nothing of this safety measure on the rainy September evening that he volunteered to get a treat for some of the Drum Corps. There was an autumn chill in the air. Cord wore a blanket swung from his shoulders on a gun strap run through its folds and fastened around his neck. It was an arrangement that had been devised by some of the men the previous winter when their overcoats had grown too ragged for comfort. But this was one night when Cord wore his blanket not so much for protection against the slashing rain as for its capacious folds which would be a good catchall for whatever he might pick up.

It was a black night. He liked the rain in his face and the sucking sound his feet made in the wet mud as he walked. He knew just what he wanted and where he could lay his hands on it, for he had seen where the sutlers had piled a fresh stock of gingerbread that afternoon. It would be easy, he thought. As he drew near the long, canvas-covered block, he saw the revenue officer disappear around the far end, some sixty feet away. Luck was with him, he felt, as he sloshed through the mud and lifted the dripping canvas. Letting it fall over him for protection, he groped along underneath until he found the boxes he was looking for.

It was but a moment's work to draw out a fine card of gingerbread and slip it into the folds of his blanket. Then he remembered a barrel of Brazil nuts nearby. These, too, slid into his blanket nicely. He had just plunged his hand in for a final fistful when he felt a heavy grip on his shoulder, through the thickness of the canvas. An angry voice began to swear at him as he squirmed helplessly under the wet curtain.

"I got yuh," the rough voice was gloating as the hand held him tight. "Ain't no use tryin' to git away! Yuh'll go straight to the Provost Marshal for this, an' I'll see yuh hung up by the thumbs—an example to all the rest of the young sneak thieves in this here thievin' army."

The man reached under the canvas and grabbed Cord by the top of his trousers. He dragged him forth and held him dangling like a helpless puppy.

"Aha! So here be the young rapscallion that's fetchin' the goods away! I saw yuh hangin' around with a hankerin' look this arternoon. Well, young fellah, me an' the Provost Marshal are gonna fix yuh so yuh'll wish't yuh'd never seed a Brazil nut!"

Cord could not have answered, even if he had known what to say. The officer had a strangling grip on him by the top of his blanket and the strap cut his throat with every long stride they took through the rain and the mud to the Provost's headquarters in the village. Major Scarritt, the Provost, was known to be a cranky old fellow with a reputation for stringing men up by the thumbs. For the second time in his army life, Cord felt really afraid.

"Now, we'll see what happens to thievin' brats in the army." The big man jerked Cord over the threshold of the Alabama House, like some kind of plunder to be laid before his chief.

"Major Scarritt," the man began, then he stopped short. Another officer sat in the Provost's chair.

Cord, roughly set upon his feet, was relieved to see that the man he faced was Major Burnett of his own regiment.

"Who—" the revenue officer began.

"Substituting," the major said, but he gave no sign of ever having seen Cord before. "What's the trouble?" he demanded curtly of the man who still held fast to Cord's collar.

"Plenty o' trouble, Major Provost Marshal, an' plenty more for this brat afore we's finished with him! I caught this young rapscallion stealin' sutlers' supplies. Got 'im red-handed, with a fistful o' Brazil nuts. Major Scarritt told me he'd make an example o' the fust thief I caught raidin' the sutlers' stores, an' here he be! I got 'im afore I'd been on the job an hour."

"Well, well, that was quick work, Officer!" smiled Major Burnett. "Better get right back and see how many more you can catch. I'll see that this fellow learns a lesson."

"String 'im up by the thumbs, Major. That's the fittest medicine for a thievin' brat like he be. An' that'll learn his chums a lesson, too, mebbe."

"Better get back to your job, Officer. That's what you're paid for, you know. I'll take care of mine."

The revenue officer stamped out of the room and slammed the door behind him. There was a silence, during which Cord felt as if he had almost stopped breathing. The major seemed quite unaware of his presence. Then at last Cord heard him speaking. His voice was stern, but he was smiling.

"Well, I guess he's gone. Now let's get down to business. Cordie Foote, how in the name of heaven did you get into a scrape like this?"

"Gosh, Major, I don't know. I just thought the boys'd like some gingerbread, and I went after it."

"Ever do it before? Nothing but the truth, young fellow!"

"No, sir, I never did. That's the honest truth, Major. I've thought about it, but I never took a thing till tonight."

The major watched him keenly, and Cord felt himself blushing under the scrutiny.

"Well, I believe you, Cord. But, after this, you'd better not think about such things. Don't you remember that poem in your school reader—

> "Vice is a monster of so frightful mien,
>   As to be hated needs but to be seen;
>   Yet seen too oft, familiar with her face,
>   We first endure, then pity, then embrace.

"In other words, it's better not to think about things you know you shouldn't do. I'll have to send you to the guardhouse, and I hope it will be a lesson to you. Remember, stealing is stealing—even from the sutlers when you're half-starved."

Cord nodded soberly.

The major called an orderly from a back room. "Take this boy to the guardhouse," he began, "and tell the sergeant—but, wait a minute!" He interrupted himself and wrote something on a slip of paper. "Give this to the sergeant of the guard. Good night, Cordie."

"Good night, sir."

Cord felt that the major would have liked to say something more to him, and there was a great deal he would like to have said to the major. But he turned and trudged away beside the orderly, feeling very small and miserable.

The guardhouse was an old brick building, much like the one they were leaving, a block farther along the muddy street. Here the sergeant of the guard greeted them gruffly. He read the note the orderly gave him with much squinting and pondering and many sidelong looks at Cord.

"Up the stairs with you, young'un. I'll be along as soon as I lay my hands on a candle."

Cord started stumbling up the stairs.

The sergeant looked at the orderly. "Major Burnett tells me not to hurt him worse than must be because he's a right decent young'un, but he tells me to teach 'im a lesson so he'll not risk stealin' again."

"What do you plan to do?"

"I'm goin' to lock 'im in with that consarned bully of a Bill Foster, and he'll never want to get in the guardhouse again."

"Hope the meanness in Bill Foster won't rub off on the young one," the orderly said.

The sergeant lit a candle and went up the stairs. Cord was waiting at the top. The door opened into a big, bare room which seemed entirely empty save for one decrepit chair on which the sergeant set the candle. Departing without a word, he locked the door behind him.

Cord stood looking at the closed door rather dazedly, then he began to inspect the room with cautious glances. Even before his eyes became adjusted to the dim light of the flickering candle, he sensed that he was not alone; then he saw a man lying on the bare floor in a far corner, apparently sound asleep. Carefully setting the candle on the floor, Cord sat down on the chair. With his head in his hands, he sat quietly for a long time. He felt shaken and bewildered, and frightened beyond all reason.

After a while he lay down on the floor, as far away as possible from his fellow prisoner. Stretching himself flat, he was bothered by the bulky army blanket which hung from his shoulders. He sat up with a jerk of annoyance to loosen the gun strap by which the blanket was fastened. The blanket dropped to the floor with a soggy plump that shook both gingerbread and nuts from its concealing folds. At almost the same moment, the man across the room sat up and rubbed his eyes.

"Hello, Bub!" he said in sleepy surprise. "Where'd you come from? Lord a'mighty, they left you a candle! Thought you'd be afeard in the dark away from your ma." He hunched himself over beside Cord and peered at him with interest. "My God, if it ain't Little Foote! Well, Footey, how'd you get in here?"

The candlelight made the man look rat-faced, with a too-long chin and too-bright eyes. Cord knew that his name was Bill Foster, but before he could say anything Bill's quick eye saw the gingerbread and the nuts.

"Oho, so that's the game! You jes knowed I like gingerbread, didn't you, Little Foote?"

He broke off a large chunk and began to eat it with ravenous bites while Cord looked on with somber indifference. When the first piece was gone, Bill broke off another which he soon swallowed with equal gusto, and another, and another, until the whole big card of gingerbread was gone. Bill's enjoyment of it spluttered forth profanely.

When he began noisily eating the nuts, Cord lay back on his blanket feeling a little sick at his stomach. Presently Bill Foster seemed to remember his presence in the room and edged a little closer to Cord. His voice was concerned now, and less mocking.

"Aw say, Footey, 'tain't nothin' to be so glum about, gettin' shut in the lockup. Come on, an' eat some o' these here pea-cans, an' let's have some fun."

"More fun to hear you eat 'em," Cord said disagreeably. "It's like gettin' sung to sleep by the daddy-mammy."

"You bet!" was the unabashed rejoinder as Bill Foster ate noisily on.

Cord determinedly shut his eyes to sleep, but his companion was not to be discouraged. Soon he tried again.

"Say, Footey, you don't wanta sleep your first night in the lockup. Won't be nothin' left for you to do later on. Now, I got a deck o' cards in my knapsack." He began to search for it as he spoke. "What d'you say to a game o' seven-up?" He slapped the cards down between them. "Ever play seven-up? If you ain't, I'll learn you."

Outside, the rain drummed on the porch roof and ran down the windowpanes, the wind moaned drearily. Inside, Cord and Bill Foster played game after game of cards, munching Brazil nuts as they played. Before the candle flickered out in a puddle of grease, Bill Foster produced another from his knapsack, and then another, until at last the gray light of dawn showed through the rain-splashed window and they both stretched out on the floor to sleep.

"'Tain't so bad in the lockup, is it, Footey?" Bill insisted, with an expansive yawn.

But Cord was too sleepy to answer.

In the course of the morning they were both released and sauntered back to camp together, Bill Foster's protecting arm across Cord's shoulders. Old Lacey and Ira Miles saw them coming and realized that something had happened to make them friends. They knew Foster to be a bully and a card sharp, and probably the worst thief in the regiment.

"What'll he do to Cordie?" Ira muttered.

Old Lacey said under his breath, "What'll Cordie do to him?"

A few nights later, near midnight, the Tenth was ordered out on a quick march to Bridgeport, ten miles to the northeast. Muffled drums sounded the call. It was a strange white night with a lopsided moon shining through rifts in the fog and shedding an eerie radiance over the rugged landscape. From dark, dripping trees the startled whippoorwills called to each other as the regiment moved through the woods in loose formation with the long strides of experienced marchers. Bill walked beside Cord.

"Gosh, Footey," he said in a hoarse voice, "I'll bet they's ghosts walkin' tonight in these here woods. Those ain't all whippoorwills acallin'—they's dead men whose bodies was left to rot, atellin' us to git along and beat the Rebs. Hear that one?" He listened as a peculiarly shrill call quavered into the night. "That ain't no bird, that's a man, a man that died in agony, an'—"

Cord felt himself beginning to shiver.

"Dry up, there!" came sternly from Ira Miles, who stepped along beside them. "Hey, Cordie, I'll beat you to that big pine tree yonder!"

They were off, but Bill kept pace with them.

"Say, Footey," he began again, when they had fallen back to their marching pace, "ever see a whippoorwill's nest?"

Cord's eyes brightened. "Can you show me one?"

"Sure, someday. If we're quiet and get close up, you can hear somethin' in his song, a sort of ticktock afore he sounds off an' a whirrin' when he finishes. Makes you think of one of those gol-derned cuckoo clocks."

The rest of the way when Cord and Bill talked at all, it was of wood lore in which Bill Foster was wise.

The moon dropped from view and the neutral light of dawn began filtering through the mist. After more than a mile of silence, Bill's talk took another turn. The two new friends were straggling along at the rear.

"Say, Footey," Bill began, "Fletcher Hughes had his pocketbook stolen this afternoon. He accused me, because I was on the detail with him for ammunition, an' they took me up to the colonel. But they couldn't prove it, so they let me go. *Why* couldn't they prove it?"

They walked along in silence. Now and again Cord stole a curious glance up at Bill. Finally he asked, "Did you steal it?"

"Sure I did, but why couldn't they prove it?"

Ira Miles dropped back to join them and Cord was glad he didn't have to try to answer Bill's question. He was too tired for one thing; and for another, they were entering Bridgeport and Cord thought he had never seen a place more beautiful.

The wide, mirror surface of the Tennessee River with the night mist still on it reflected the blue rim of surrounding mountains between shadowy tree-lined banks. Only the mutilated skeleton of the railroad bridge destroyed by the Confederates in retreat to Chattanooga—its stone piers trailing strands of twisted metal to riffle the calm, strong current —bore witness that the peaceful landscape harbored warring armies bent upon destruction. Someone pointed out Lookout Mountain, pivotal landmark of the campaign. In the wild country that spread between where the Tenth was standing and where Lookout kept its vigil over Chattanooga, the men knew that every ford or cove or mountain pass was significant. In it, three great corps of Union soldiers were feeling their way by different routes to Chattanooga. The enemy, by any one of a dozen movements, might bottle up different detachments and starve them into surrender.

"It sure is beautiful," Ira Miles murmured, "but it sure is menacing."

Cord felt a tingle of excitement running up his spine. They were on the edge of battle. Nothing could turn them back now. Even the Tenth's military duty of guarding the cracker line could no longer seem dull when at any moment the enemy, using the secret resources of the mountains they knew so well and aided by the prevailing mists of the autumn, might encircle them. Cord's trusty slingshot was in his pocket. He never doubted but that he could use it on other than small game if there was need; but he wished that he had a gun.

After a brief rest in Bridgeport, the regiment was scattered on various details. Companies D and F were dispatched to picket a shallow ford, seven miles down the river, where a lazy stream called Widow's Creek meandered in to the Tennessee over sandy shoals between bordering cane brakes. Here they camped for more than a week, building themselves ingenious shelters out of the sugar cane that grew in rank profusion down to the water's edge. Here Bill Foster put a gun in Cord's hands and taught him how to use it. They went on hunting expeditions into the woods, shooting rabbit and small game which Bill showed Cord how to stew in his coffeepot. They feasted and swam in the river and sunned themselves on its banks, unaware of the tragic events that were taking place across the Tennessee and beyond the outer mountains of Chattanooga; unaware, yet always ready for the orders that might come any day. Cord had practiced, until his fingers could perform in his sleep, the battle calls that would send the men of his company into action.

"Uncase the colors!" "Sound the drums!" "Blow the charge!" were words he longed to hear.

First news of the battle of Chickamauga reached Companies D and F from a family of refugees, a very old man, his wife and their married daughter, who came through the ford in an ancient cart drawn by an equally ancient horse. They had been burned out by bushwhackers, they said, because the daughter's husband had fought in the Union army. All that had been left to them of their farm possessions was the old horse and cart. The elderly woman lay on a feather bed in the back of the cart, but her husband sat sturdily beside his daughter. It was she who had got them all finally to safety, leading or driving the aged horse all the way from Lemore's Cove, through Cooper's Gap and Trenton, sometimes walking many miles on the steep mountain roads, sleeping on the ground wrapped in a blanket underneath the cart. They were all exhausted, and said they could never have got so far had it not been for the kindness of Union soldiers in directing them and sharing with them their meager rations. Stevenson was their goal.

The old man was garrulous with grief. "My father went through Valley Forge with George Washington," he told the captain.

The men of the two companies crowded around to hear the epic lament. Cord, squirming among the soldiers, got himself into the front row, as close as he could to the refugees.

"My father brought me out from Virginia by Cumberland Gap as a lad of six," the old man went on, "and I fought with Andy Jackson in 1812. Nary I thought to see the day when a man would be burned out of house and land because he loves his country. Why, sir, the Union was my father's religion!"

Two days later, a string of terrified Negroes came through, leading a lame mule which they took turns riding.

"Oh, massey," the leader of them wailed, "the Yankees we wuz diggin' wells fo' got all shot to pieces, an' ef we'uns git kotched, we'uns'll sho' be hanged."

No one could make anything intelligible of their frightened chatter as the captain sent them on to Stevenson.

"Who's winnin' this war anyway?" George Jay asked glumly.

Old Lacey turned on him sharply. "We'll know when the Michigan Tenth gets into action."

That night there was a heavy rainstorm, with thunder and lightning so violent that the great battle they all knew was imminent might have been upon them. A rush of waters from the flooding river swept away their fragile cane shelters. The men had to move hurriedly to higher ground, in the rain-lashed dark, or they and their possessions would have been swept away.

The next morning as they tried vainly to dry themselves beside fires which would not burn, a messenger came from Bridgeport with orders to return there at once. The Second Brigade, of which they were a unit, had been dispatched to Anderson's Cross Roads, sixty miles to the north. The men plied the orderly with questions before he rode away. Yes, he told them, there had been a terrible battle . . . not a smashing defeat, but not a victory either . . . General Thomas had really saved the day, with part of the Fourteenth Corps. "Stood like a rock against half the Rebel army. They're calling him 'the Rock of Chickamauga,' " the orderly said, as he touched his spurs to his horse and rode off to Bridgeport.

Cord let his eyes dwell for a moment on the hump in the blue horizon which was Lookout Mountain. Somewhere off that way lay Chickamauga. He was glad the Fourteenth had done itself proud, and that General Thomas was a hero. Perhaps the rest of them were on their way to join him now and would have their chance to be heroes, too.

They floundered toward Bridgeport through the treacherous red mud that was unbelievably sticky and slippery. More than once Cord lost his footing and slid headlong into a roadside puddle. When Companies D and F reached Bridgeport, they were plastered with mud almost beyond recognition. At that very moment, coming in by rail from Florence, was General Hooker's Eleventh Corps from the Army of the Potomac. The mud-bedraggled pickets from Widow's Creek Ford stood gaping by the roadside when the Easterners marched past smartly, washed and shaved, with clean collars, shining arms, polished buttons, blanket rolls neatly strapped on their shoulders, accoutrements in order.

"Look at the brass-button dudes with their paper collars!" Bill Foster shouted out.

Others joined in.

"Hey, would you jump if your nice shiny guns went off?"

"Would you cry if your faces got dirty?"

"Look out there, Percy, you might get some mud on your boots!"

"Shut up, you dirty bums!" one of the Easterners retorted.

East and West might banter about appearance but every man was ready to prove his mettle in battle. Jeers soon turned to cheers and before anyone knew what was happening someone from the Army of the Cumberland or the Army of the Potomac started to sing:

> "We'll rally round the flag, boys, we'll rally
>   once again,
> Shouting the battle cry of Freedom."

And soon all were singing as one mighty group of men.

CHAPTER VII

It was noon of the next day when Companies F and D came up with their regiment, sloshing along through the mud and singing one of their favorite songs:

> "I'm Captain Jinks, of the Horse Marines;
> I feed my horse on corn and beans,
> And sport young ladies in their teens,
> Though a captain in the army.
> I teach young ladies how to dance,
> How to dance, how to dance,
> I teach young ladies how to dance,
> For I'm the pet of the army."

Slogging along the road by the river, sometimes waist-deep in water, they were a muddy-looking horde but a hilarious one and they roared out the chorus with gusto:

> "Captain Jinks of the Horse Marines;
> I feed my horse on corn and beans,
> And often live beyond my means,
> Though a captain in the army."

It was a beautiful countryside through which they marched, except for the mud from the recent rain, and that they took in their stride. The October woods were golden, and the October scent was in the air.

Late in the day Cord found himself trudging at the rear beside Old Lacey, who had begun to feel the strain of the long marches. "Let's stop and rest a bit, Pop. We can catch up with 'em easy."

Old Lacey assented, and they stretched themselves on a leafy bank above the roadside. It had been hard going since Widow's Creek. At Bridgeport they had crossed the river by raft and walked the railroad five miles to Love's Ferry, where they crossed again and pushed well up into the Sequatchie valley before camping for the night. Today they had come a good fifteen miles farther.

"What do you think we're headin' for, Pop?" Cord asked.

"Hard to tell, Cordie, hard to tell. Somethin' pretty bad is my guess. They say all the cavalry the Johnnies have got is gallopin' toward Anderson's Cross Roads to cut off the cracker line to Chattanooga."

Cord would have welcomed a cavalry charge just then. He could picture the enemy plunging over the hill with the Tenth rushing to meet them, bayonets fixed and all of them shouting at the tops of their voices "Captain Jinks of the Horse Marines."

That there had been a cavalry charge only the day before was soon evident. The marching men of the Tenth first became aware of it as the early dusk was falling when a faint, sickish odor came to them on a rising wind from the north. It grew stronger and more pungent as they pushed along, too tired now to sing, but determined to reach their goal before stopping for the night. As they crested the last high hill, the odor became a horrible stench.

"Dead mules!" gasped Old Lacey.

Scouts, riding back, reported to the advance guard that the road ahead was completely blocked by the wreck of a wagon train. Orders were given to drop back over the hill and camp for the night in battle formation, ready for whatever might come. No one came to the Union camp that night except two frightened muleteers who had escaped Rebel capture at the time of the attack and had been hiding in the woods.

"They're plain devils, I tell ye, nothin' human coulda done it! You'll see," one of them blurted out, still shuddering with the horror of his experience.

"They rode sideways along the gulch, up on one side and back on t'other, shootin' the mules an' screechin' that savage yell o' theirs an' tellin' us to run for our lives," the other said wildly.

"Then they come burnin' the wagons, an' druv us poor fellas up the valley. We'uns here got away when an ammunition wagon blowed up an' killed a mess of 'em. But what was that to ten thousand! I tell ye there musta ben ten thousand easy," he insisted shrilly.

The other placed his estimate at two thousand.

The officers agreed that was more likely, being about the number in General Joe Wheeler's famous cavalry brigade.

Numbers became meaningless when, in the uncertain light of early morning with the drummers doing their best to bestir the men, the Tenth saw the actual carnage. It blocked the road and spilled over into fields and woodlands. Charred remainders of three hundred wagons blackened the meadow below them and splotched the narrow defile which the road became as it climbed the steep ascent of Walden's Ridge and dropped down to Anderson's Cross Roads. The scorched bodies of eighteen hundred mules lay where they had fallen.

The immediate task of the brigade was to dispose of the dead mules. Men were set to work digging long, deep trenches to bury them in. Others heaped those nearest into a huge pyre, poured kerosene on it, and set it on fire. But after one great blaze there was no more kerosene, and the sodden carcasses would not burn without it.

"There are eighteen hundred mules to be buried at the rate of three hundred a day," Old Lacey said to the Drum Corps. "Hang up your drums, boys, and get a spade in your hands, or the nearest thing you can find to one. Everyone's needed on this job."

LEGEND
——·——·—— STATE BORDERS
— — — — — — CORYDON FOOTE
~~~~~~~~~ RIVERS

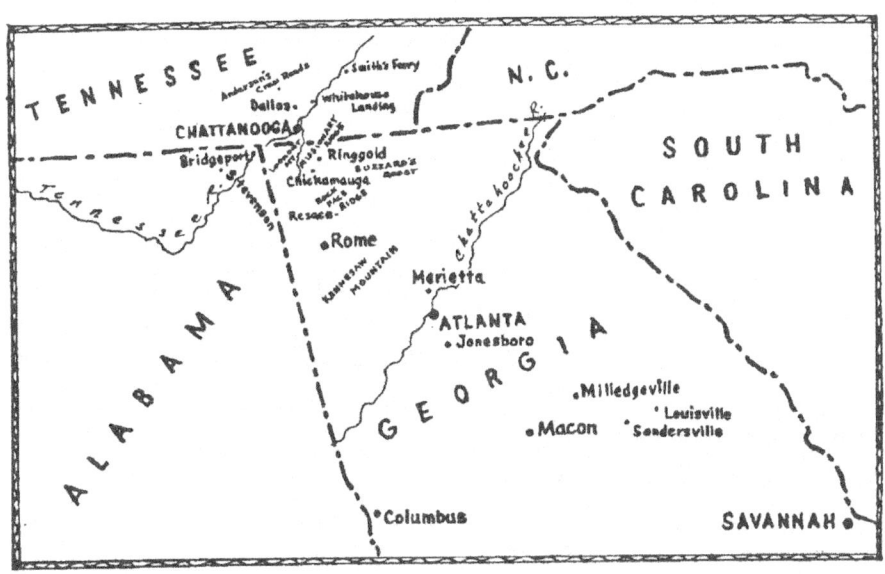

CAMPAIGNING WITH THE MICHIGAN 10 TH INFANTRY
1862 – 1865
II

Cord, who had thought to be fighting Rebels by now, was engaged in burying mules. He hoped there would be some other news to report before he wrote his next letter home.

Other crews were hard at work clearing the road of charred debris while an empty wagon train from Chattanooga awaited its turn to cross over at the eastern base of the ridge. On the second day a full supply train came toiling up from Stevenson and Bridgeport with Lieutenant Tom Branch riding his prancing black at the fore and Tommy coming up behind on his small gray donkey. Cord dropped his spade and ran to meet him.

"So they haven't sent you home!"

"Not me," Tommy replied with a swagger. "D'you think I want to leave the war before we've licked the Johnnies? But I gave your eggs and the cartridge belt and the box to Captain Hart when he went back to Flint last month."

Cord smiled his thanks, relieved to know that some of his treasures were safe at home by now.

Old Lacey, seeing the boys together, gave Cord time off from digging for the rest of the day. The boys soon headed for the woods. These were new to Cord but the countryside was familiar to Tommy from frequent stops made in the vicinity with the wagon train. There were many places he wanted to show to Cord. One was a plum orchard where late plums grew as large as peaches. Another was a chestnut grove where the nuts were already dropping. In it they found a pair of wild hogs making their lair. They watched them for a while, then Tommy's foraging instinct asserted itself.

"Gosh, Cordie, if we only had a gun we could have a barbecue!"

Cord thought for a moment. "I bet I know a fellow'll give us a gun."

When approached that night, Bill Foster was agreeable, and did not ask too many questions. Next morning, as he walked with the boys to the edge of the woods, he asked, "What do I get for it, Footey?"

"Best meal you've had this side of the Ohio!" boasted Cord.

"That's not sayin' much."

"You wait an' see."

Bill left them and the boys scrambled up the ridge alone, Cord carrying the gun. As they neared the chestnut grove, Tommy said, "I know you got the gun, Cordie, but I got the hog. I wish't I could shoot him."

Cord had been counting on doing that himself but, after all, it was Tommy's hog.

"Well, I'll show you, Tommy, and you can have the first shot anyway."

Tommy was quick at the business of learning the sights and the trigger. After prowling about a bit they decided to lie in wait behind a fallen tree on which they could rest the gun, pointed into the leafy trench the hogs had made. After a long hour of lying in suspense, a big ragged fellow came grunting forth. Tommy sighted calmly and pulled the trigger. As the shot crashed, Tommy went over backwards. The hog, with a shrill screech, rolled over on its side and after a moment lay still.

"You got 'im! You got 'im!" shrieked Cord, racing over to the animal. "You got 'im clean! The bullet went straight through him lengthways."

"Jimminy," said Tommy dazedly, as he picked himself up, "I thought I was at the wrong end o' the gun."

"You gotta get used to the kick," Cord told him, realizing then that he had forgotten to tell Tommy what Bill Foster had made so clear to him.

Together they dragged the animal to the edge of the grove and set about to skin it, as Cord had learned to skin a rabbit the week before when hunting with Bill. But a hog and a rabbit seemed to be strangely different creatures. Two hours of gory struggle followed before the boys tied the feet of the carcass together as they had seen at butcher shops, hung them over a stout limb, and started carrying it back to camp.

As they came out of the chestnut grove, Cord stopped suddenly. "Listen, Tommy," he whispered, "there's the other one! I bet I can get 'im."

He backed against a tree, sighted deliberately, and fired. The hog rolled over, shrieking, but subsided with a second shot. They decided not to skin their second hog.

"We'll see how Wardie Fisher does it before we try another."

They inched their way down the steep path with their first prize. Bill Foster was watching for them and went back to help them get the second hog, quite as pleased as they were at their prowess. Under Wardie Fisher's skilled hand, there was a barbecue that night. The savory fragrance of roasting meat filled the air. It was the first fresh pork the men had tasted since they had left home eighteen months before. The boys brought chestnuts to roast, and rutabagas. Wild plums and crab apples completed the feast.

"Forage never tasted better." Old Lacey smiled.

They needed the strength of that good meal, for heavy rains came and though the road was clear again there was the further task of getting loaded wagons over the ridge. The mud was not only deep, it sometimes seemed bottomless. Days followed during which, for all the tugging and shouting and pushing and digging, they could not get more than twenty wagons over the ridge between daylight and dark.

When they finally made camp a few days later at Anderson's Cross Roads, the good news was awaiting them that Colonel McCook's cavalry had driven back General Joe Wheeler's brigade across the Tennessee toward Knoxville, beating them in two sharp encounters.

The Tenth was given two days off detail. They needed

time to get their equipment in order again, and some of the men needed it to write long-deferred letters home. Cord made the most of his two days.

> Anderson Cross Roads
> East Tennesee Oct 16th

Dear Parents I received your kind letter dated the 2nd and was very glad to hear from as it had been some time since I heard from you. I received your other letter but we were ordered to march and I did not have time to answer it, and we did not get our knapsacks till 3 days and when I got my tent up I got a letter from will and Abby and one from George Turner and by the time I got them answered it Commenced to rain and rained 3 days Steady and today for the first time I have an Oppertunity to answer your letter we are Camped in Sequatche Vally on the Anderson Cross Rorads 411 Miles South of nowhere and on half raitions and only part Rations to boot and no knowing when we will be able to get any more through for the Rail-Road is Cut off and the rains has made the road so muddy that it is almost impossible to get waggons over them and it is one mass of waggons Clear through to bridgeport for Rosey has to have his Army Supplied with Waggons and that makes it bad for us 3 Companys. A F & D are on detail to help waggons over the mountain it is a large mountain and the men have to help the Waggons over it is where a large suply train was burnt you have in all probability heard of it the Estimate of waggons burnt is Calculated at about 6 hundred and I do not think it is over Estimated, Either for I see them myself I wish you could seen them some of them had Just Harnessed up and was waiting to move when they Came down on them they shot the mules in their harness but did not kill the men on them I see six mules in the harness Just as they were shot down. they took one critter up the mountain and pounded him most to death he Came out pretty well they said they did not Intend to kill any of our men the Col of the 1st Wisconsin Cav killed two rebels and wounded 3 with his Sabre. I see one Rebbel major he wounded he marked him nice he cut him across upper part of his lip between his nose and lip Clear across his face. we are now transfered to the 3rd Brigade 2nd Division 14th Aramy Corps mogan Comdg Brigade J C. Davis Comdg Division Thomas Comdg Corps Lew wells is well and sends his respects to you. you wanted me to give you a description of the people and their looks and manners. they are Generally—the female Sex— tall raw boned and long siff har uncomed and old home spun dresses ragged and dirty and generally go barefooted and very Coarse uncouth manners and generally no Education. they live in log houses and some of them have them boarded up and shingled with Shakes the men are about the sam with some Exceptions there I think I have given you a good Description of the people and now I will give you a Desription of the Country it is generally very mountainious and rockey and the only good farming land is in the vally and that is Splended. there is some splended timber here generaly chestnut and walnut with some oak and maple. I must tell you of a little Incident that occured in Company H last night 4 of them went across the river a foraging and killed 2 big hogs and made a raft and when they was comeing back across the river the raft came to pieces and let them and the hogs into the watter. 2 of them could swim and 2 could not the 2 that could swim got out all right but the other 2 went down stream they sent a detail down after them and about 2 miles they found one who hung to a rail and paddled ashore and the other one caught a tree and got out of the water but did not get out of the tree. he set in the tree and hollered like a Screech Owl all night he was wet and set in all one cold night to pay for killing a hog and lost his hog to boot. you said that Flecther Servis said they did not make Charlie Gardner go into the Fight. they make all the musicians go in the fights in this Regiment. you believe in Sir John Fallstaffs Doctrine—he that from battle run away will live to

Fight another day But he that is in battle Slain will never live to Fight again. I think it is very True. I have received the weekly very Regular and I am getting very much inerted in the Storys Especially in the Bride of Death and Showns the Greek. I got a letter from Ally the same day I got the one from you I am sorry of one thing in Alley he says he has learned to Chew and Smoke. if he Could have the Chance to see the affect of it I do he would quit I know for it I think it is one of the worst Habbits in the world and shall always try and avoid it. I think by our desription of my Heifer she must be a beauty. and I want you to keep my Bantees good and tell me how they get along once in a while. and how the boys and girles get along and give my respects to them all and tell them I am right side up with care yet and will always try and be so while I am in the Army I am very sorry Mrs. Bennett is sick and tell her I am gointo write soon and I haint forgot that nice Cake she baked for me and wish I had another. I do not think there is any Chance to get a box through to me now as we are not where the cars can reach us now but if we are I will give due Information. I heard of Col Mecrary being killed or taken Prisoner and Mr Aramstrong see Mr Hopkins but I did not get a chance to see him. he Must have been Col of the 22nd for they was in the Fight and got cut up badly Lew has got better now and is on duty now. that was bad for Miss Benton I declare. you said to try the white of an egg on Lew we have not seen an egg in a dogs age. I think the most direct route to me now is to direct to Bridgeport Alabama and it will come. you want me to Commence a Journal you do not know how it is here. we ar some times on the march and do not get our knap sacks and then we do not camp untill sun down and then get supper and I feel like haveing a napp till morning and get up at 4 or five in the morning. aint what it is cracked up to be you know. you must send me Stamps this time and on for I depend on you for Stamps we cant get any here for love or money. I have got me a tent by myself now and I made a nice desk to write on annd a Stool to set on and have every thing my own way now I cannot think of any thing more Just now but I will wait till in the morning and finish my letter.

I am now agointo to take the Opertunity to finish my letter.

me and Lew Wells and 3 others went up the mountain and got all of the Cestnuts we could Eat. I cannot think any thing more this time only Mr. Louks sends you and Mr. Carrier his Best Respects and hopes you are well one of them men who killed the hog is fined 10 dollars and 10 days work on the Breast Works hard Labor. rough on him. no more this time from your affectionate son.

CORIDON .E. FOOTE,
Anderson Cross
Roads

P.S. when you write to
   Aunty Foote tell her
      to write to me and give her
         my Address
            C. E. F.

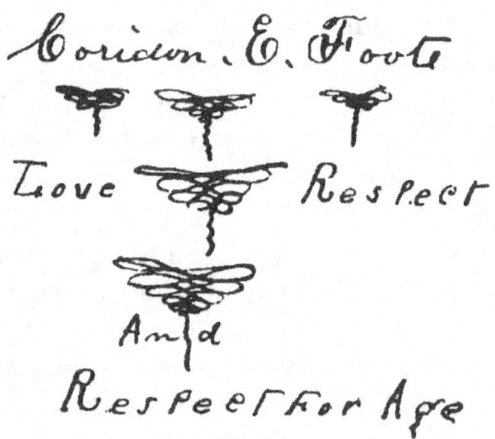

He drew from a folder in his knapsack the pictures they had sent him from time to time—his mother and father, his brother Will, all but Hannah, and they had said they were sending one of her soon. He wished they had sent him something by Captain Hart when he returned from Flint, but they had not. He was glad for the weeklies that reached him fairly regularly, and for the clothes they had sent to him a short time ago, but he was especially glad to have their likenesses. He decided to add another line to his letter.

> PS Mr Louks sends his love and he very well all is well you know here.
>
> CORD

When orders came for a part of the brigade at Anderson's to move to Smith's Ferry for patrol duty on the northern Tennessee—where it was thought the enemy might attempt a return—the Tenth Michigan and the Sixtieth Illinois, with the Fifth Wisconsin Artillery, were dispatched for the job.

It was almost beyond horse and human power to get the guns over the mountains. For three days they struggled, mostly in driving rain. One company was assigned to each gun. They urged, coaxed and flogged the horses and mules as they strained and floundered until it seemed quivering flesh could endure no more. Yet these same roads, roundabout and hazardous as they might be, were the only route of supplies between Stevenson and Chattanooga, for Rebel guns had been planted to sweep every approach that was more direct. Should the tenuous cracker line be broken at any point in its hundred and ten difficult miles, the army which now occupied Chattanooga would be starved into surrender.

As the Tenth labored along toward Dallas, Tennessee, Cord began to understand why Lieutenant Tom now bore his responsibility so soberly. Breakdowns were frequent on the narrow mountain roads, and a breakdown meant complete blockade until repairs could be made. For six miles behind, drivers chafed and swore as they waited on precarious hillsides with their patient beasts shank-deep in mud. Every delay meant diminished rations, and diminished rations meant further delay; scores of mules now dropped daily in their tracks, too weak with hunger to struggle longer on the terrible roads.

After five days of marching they arrived at Dallas and were greeted with the news that General Rosecrans was to be removed and General Thomas advanced to his place. Cumberlanders were loyal to their first commanding general, in spite of the year of comparatively small achievement, and there was a hush of sadness among them when General Rosecrans' farewell was read:

> The general commanding, in taking leave of you, his brothers in arms, officers and soldiers, congratulates you that your new commander comes to you not as he did, a stranger. General Thomas has been identified with this army from its first organization. He has led you often in battle. To his known prudence, dauntless courage, and true patriotism, you may look with confidence that under God he will lead you to victory. The general commanding doubts not that you will be as true to yourselves and your country in the future as you have been in the past. Companions in arms, officers and soldiers, farewell, and may God bless you.

Impatient citizens in the north, reading their newspapers at comfortable firesides, might censure General Rosecrans for not moving faster, but the men of the Cumberland, close to the daily difficulties and overwhelming odds that confronted him, were slower to judge. The soldiers at Dallas that night, all from units of the Fourteenth Corps, were comforted in the fact that if General Rosecrans must go, their own corps commander, General Thomas, had been found worthy to succeed him. The men had further satisfaction in the announcement that General Grant was at Chattanooga in high command of all armies.

"Well, if Grant can get us through this cursed red mud any faster, here's to Grant!" was Old Lacey's comment, as the Tenth set forth again northward the next day.

After four difficult days, they reached Smith's Ferry near midnight of the 25th of October. Cord could scarcely wait for morning to come, to discover in daylight what darkness concealed. He was out and at his post early, first of the drummers for reveille, as if the mere act of drumming would bring the daylight faster. When the sun shone, a welcome warmth came into the air. Cord decided that he liked Smith's Ferry, and the sound his drum was making relayed the feeling to others.

The river was wide, its banks wooded and low. They were camped within the arc of a deep bend more than a mile in extent. This was some two miles below the point where the main road from Washington divided, with one branch leading to Harrison and the other to Georgetown and Cleveland, crossing at ferries a mile and a half apart. These ferries were to be guarded now by the guns of the Fifth Wisconsin, the guns that had been so painfully transported up and over the mountain ridges. All along the river on either side of the Tenth's campground, for two miles or more, infantry regiments were soon encamped.

General Joe Wheeler's cavalry was known to be almost directly across the river. Sniping between the two armies was frequent at first, and desultory firing occurred each day. But gradually, as Indian summer sunshine poured beneficently upon them all, a kind of mutual truce came into effect along the river. Men grew less cautious and more curious about each other. Foraging was good, and swimming too. They relaxed in the autumn sunshine and a fellow feeling for their enemies began to develop among the men of the Union brigades.

One afternoon, as Cord and Bill Foster and George Jay lay sunning themselves at the river's edge after a long swim, a bullet whistled past them. As they scurried for cover, laughter sounded from across the river.

"Better look out, Yanks, we'll get you next time!" a mocking voice called.

Bill Foster came out from behind a tree and deliberately turned a handspring in full view of the enemy. "Just see if you can, Johnny, I give you leave!" he called back, equally mocking.

"Too easy, Yank."

A day or two later, when the three were again near the same place, a voice called to them from across the river, "Hey, Yanks!"

They alerted, but made no answer.

"Hey, Yanks, we want to talk to you, Yanks!"

"Talk away, Johnnies," answered George Jay, "our ears is cocked."

Three youths in gray came out from the trees on the other side and laid down their guns as one called, rather more cautiously than before, "Say, Yanks, if we told you where to find a boat, would you come over?"

The three looked at each other in consternation, then Bill Foster answered for them. "Sure we would, Johnnies! Where's the boat?"

"A few turns up the way you're goin', tied to a tree. We'll meet you up there."

"Are you straight?" Bill challenged.

"Straight as they're made!"

"You'll sure get hell if you ain't."

They set forth in great haste up the river to find the boat, Cord and George somewhat uneasily, Bill in bright-eyed excitement.

"Don't forget, Bill," Cord ventured, "they're the fellows that made the awful mess at Anderson's."

"Gosh, that's why I like 'em, Footey! That was a hell of a sweet job. I couldn't a' done a better one myself."

They found the boat, a crude dugout, with a pair of oars.

True to their promise, the Johnnies appeared across the river. Bill took the oars and rowed his two somewhat frightened companions to the other side. Three slender youths in worn gray uniforms were waiting to greet them.

"Hello, Yanks, you're good sports. We didn't think you'd do it."

"Is that what you want to talk about?" snapped Bill.

"Oh, no," their spokesman answered genially, "we just got tired snipin' at you across the river an' thought we'd like to get acquainted."

"You ain't such crack shots at that!"

Bill was inclined to be suspicious, and Cord and George gazed at the Rebs diffidently.

"No, we could do better," one of the boys in gray continued, lazily.

"You know damn well we can get you when we half try!" another flared.

"Sure," the third added, pacifying his fellows, "but we're sick of it, Yanks, sick of it, and most pow'ful hungry. How about you?"

"There's good rabbits around here," Cord said. "I got a dandy, yesterday."

"Yeah, but what's a rabbit without any salt! You got any salt or any coffee you want to trade for tobacco?"

Bill was suddenly all business. "Not for tobacco, Johnny, but I'll give you all the salt you want for good Yankee money."

"Honest to goodness?"

"Honest to goodness. Meet me here tomorrow, Johnny. I'll bring you a bottle of salt—so high"—he measured off five inches—"and you can have it for two-fifty, Yankee money."

"Lord a'mighty, man, where d'you think we can get that much Yankee money?"

They dickered awhile, but finally Bill's proposition stood.

"See you tomorrow, Johnnies, same time," Bill said, and they were off across the river and a race back to camp before roll call.

Bill did not take Cord and George into his confidence as to plans for the next day, but he came around for them when it was time to start up the river. When they reached the dugout, they saw the boys in gray waiting for them on the opposite shore.

"Hello, Yanks, come on over!"

"All right, Johnnies, we'll be there." Bill oared the dugout as fast as he could across the wide, still river while Cord and George wondered breathlessly what was going to happen.

"I feel sorry for you, Yank, if you didn't bring that salt."

"Not half as sorry as I feel for you, if you haven't got that money, Johnny."

"Well, here's your money, Yank, and a pow'ful lot of it for that little bottle o' salt!"

Bill held tight to the mustard bottle filled with salt as he examined the money in the Southerner's outstretched hand. "It's real," he decided. "How'd you get it—sell Jeff Davis's mule?"

"No, Abe Lincoln's filly. But say, Yank, let's taste the stuff in that bottle before you get your money."

Bill removed the cork and held the bottle toward the boy in gray, who poked in a finger and tasted.

"Lordy, it's real!" he yelled with delight. Slapping the money into Bill's hand, he snatched the bottle from him and danced about, shouting to his fellows, "Taste it, Jim! Taste it, Dunny! It's real!"

Suspicion and enmity were forgotten. Blue and gray sat on a log and asked each other questions about their homes and their families, then they speculated on how long the war might last.

Presently it was time for the Michigan soldiers to race back to camp for evening roll. When they had crossed the river and tied up the dugout, a taunting voice sang out, "Look out, Yanks, we're goin' to shoot!"

"Shoot away, Johnnies!" Bill picked up his gun which he had left beside a tree before they crossed the river. He fired at random. "Shoot away, but let me know when you want some more salt."

"They're pretty good fellows," Cord admitted.

"Would be," Bill agreed, "if they didn't think they're smarter 'n God."

Bill was in the salt business, taking Yankee money when he could get it and when he could not there was always tobacco which he sold to the sutlers. His source of supply remained a mystery until the day he and Cord were foraging along the lower river.

"See that old shed over there, Footey?" Bill pointed to a dilapidated outbuilding near a deserted farmhouse. "That's where I found my salt mine. Ran onto a whole barrel o' the stuff the second day I was here. Rolled it over into the woods that night and buried it. Sure is a regular salt mine."

"'Bout made your fortune with it, haven't you, Bill?"

"Sure have, Footey. Look out, there's a rabbit."

As the warm days drowsed on, Yanks and Johnnies all along the river grew increasingly friendly.

"Say, Johnnies, let's stop shootin' an' go for a swim," the call would go forth.

"All right, Yanks!"

Presently, rival pickets would be sporting together in midstream, but always they kept a sharp lookout for scouting lieutenants. Cord tried to puzzle out how it was that they could have so much fun with people one day when the next day they did their best to kill them.

"'Tisn't the people," George Jay said, "it's just the war."

But that didn't make sense to Cord.

Bill Foster was the one man who was finally caught and punished for fraternizing with the enemy. Cord found him one day lying outside his captain's tent, bucked and gagged —his knees tied up to his chin and a stick fastened between his teeth. Bill looked up at him beseechingly, but a sentry was coming so Cord could only get out of the way. Later in the day, Cord met up with Bill again, free now.

"Sorry I couldn't get you untangled this morning, Bill," Cord began with a grin.

"Forget it," snapped Bill. "Come on for a swim."

They strolled off together. Down the river a little way Bill drew a shining revolver from his pocket, fondled it a moment, and then gave it to Cord. "Ain't she a beauty, Footey? Look at the printin' on her."

Cord found himself holding a handsome, gold-mounted revolver. On the handle was engraved:

> To Captain Noah H. Hart,
> from his friends in Lapeer

"Gosh, Bill, where'd you get it?" Cord asked, in awe.

"I found it in the captain's boodoir," Bill minced. Then, taking the shining weapon from Cord's hands, he said, "But I reckon the captain will never leave it lay in his boodoir again." Bill hurled it as far as his strength would carry it out over the Tennessee. It dropped with a plump into the quiet current. "There, that gets us even! Now, let's go swimmin'."

When November frosts crimsoned the landscape, winds soon came to sweep its glory away. The Tenth received a message from the high command. "The Tenth Michigan Infantry and the Sixtieth Illinois Infantry will proceed to Chattanooga at once, under light marching orders," said the hard-riding orderly. "The Fifth Wisconsin Artillery and wagon trains to follow with all dispatch."

The words sang in their ears as they packed their light

equipment and the drums beat out the call to assembly. Through most of the day the drums sounded. By nightfall the Tenth was on the march, with their blankets rolled snugly, three days' cooked rations in their haversacks, and forty rounds of ammunition in their cartridge belts.

"This means a battle, sure," Old Lacey said to them.

It was sixty miles to their destination, over rough roads. On the evening of the third day, by the rising of the moon, they marched into White House Landing, just four crow-miles above Chattanooga. It was a cold, still night. Campfires flared in the mist all about them and men could be seen tramping before them, thrashing their arms for warmth. The Tenth soon found other units of their division which had come in under similar orders. General Davis, their division commander, rode by with General Morgan, who had come down with the rest of the brigade they had left at Anderson's Cross Roads. Men kept coming into camp, and still more men, marching in quietly from the surrounding night and disappearing again into the darkness where soon new campfires could be seen flaring feebly through the mist. Everywhere was order and precision. No drums sounded, only the muffled footfalls of marching men echoed against the stillness.

That was the night of a nearly total eclipse of the moon. Men watched it fearfully, and superstition was rampant through the camps.

"Awful bad luck," wailed Bill Foster, "awful bad luck to start anything like a battle the day after an eclipse."

"Bad luck for who?"

"Bad luck for the fellow that starts it."

Cord was gazing up toward the heights of Missionary Ridge where enemy campfires shone dimly through the mist. "Well, it's bad luck for the Johnnies then," he reasoned. "They started this war, and besides, they're nearest the moon."

CHAPTER VIII

SOMETIME AFTER MIDNIGHT, in the early morning hours before the great battles of Chattanooga began, Cord and George, unable to sleep, slipped out for a prowl. The eclipse was past, and a moon nearly full shed a mist-muted radiance through the night, lighting their way through the woods to the river. Close to the tree-lined margin of the river, pontoon boats were moored which were being quickly and quietly manned by soldiers, each of whom carried a spade and a gun. Among them moved a smallish man wearing a slouch hat and an ulster who spoke quiet words here and there, intent and concerned and kindly. One by one the boats slipped away down the current without telltale splash of oars, until he stood alone on the riverbank with two companions. There was nothing to mark him as an officer, except the way he gave commands.

"D'you suppose it's Uncle Billy?" George whispered.

"Mebbe it is." Cord nodded.

If it was, they were seeing General Sherman at the great moment of sending his advance guard over the river to prepare for the crossing of the armies to the assault on Missionary Ridge.

"Can't say why," George said, still whispering, "but I'd do most anything that man told me to do, go 'most anywhere...."

Back in their tent again, after a little sleep, the boys were wakened by the passing of marching men, regiment after regiment moving toward the river. The men might have been ghosts walking, for all the sound they made—no talk, no orders, just steady rhythm and movement, out of the mist behind, into the mist ahead. Even the sound of their feet was gone the moment the mist swallowed them.

Orders came at daylight for their own unit to march in the same direction. No drums were to be sounded. Brief commands, swiftly given, were to be carried out with all possible speed and a minimum of noise. When the Tenth got under way, the boys felt as if they were marching into misty nothingness, as the other regiments had when they had seen them going by their tent. Reaching the river's edge, they found a newly completed pontoon bridge, straw-covered to silence their feet, extending toward the fog-hidden opposite shore.

Once on the other side, they were lined up as reserves along the banks of the Chickamauga River near its emptying into the Tennessee. Here the engineers were building another pontoon bridge. To see it grow was a wonderful thing, and Cord watched fascinated as pontoon after pontoon swung into place with fine precision. Planks laid down across them at the instant of their anchoring were clamped into position, side by side, end to end, men working noiselessly in a rhythm which scarcely erred or altered, until a wide, clean highway thirteen hundred and fifty feet long spanned the Tennessee River.

From their vantage point as reserves that day, the boys watched a stirring panorama that stretched away before them through rugged woodland and upward into the mist that lay along the heights of Missionary Ridge. There was drizzling rain; and low-hanging clouds so completely cloaked the movements of the advancing columns from the sight of the enemy that they were able to push far up along the foothills at the end of the ridge without opposition. When, shortly after noon, there came the sound of distant firing, the boys knew that the great clash had begun in other sections if not their own, and they strained their eyes vainly to see through the veil of clouds and mist. For two hours the roll of cannon and crackle of musketry continued, echoing among the shrouded hills. Then a rising wind tore away the fog for a time and they could see the faraway, pygmy progress of men in blue straight up the face of Lookout Mountain toward its cloud-wrapped summit. Cheer after cheer burst from the reserves as they watched.

Cord knew then that he could never forget the sight of that gallant line of blue moving up the slope . . . of the color-bearer who scrambled over the rocks ahead of the rest . . . of the officer calling, "Bring the colors back to the men!" and the man shouting back, "Bring the men up to the colors!" Then the fog closed in again and enemy guns began to thunder on Missionary Ridge just above them.

The reserves turned to watch the progress of columns near at hand, though even their maneuvers were often mist-hidden. Firing continued for more than an hour, stopping only as the early dusk dropped down. No one could say what the outcome had been until an orderly brought the welcome news that General Hooker's men had captured Lookout Mountain.

"And the troops on the ridge?"

"No one knows yet."

Meanwhile, the wind was fast blowing the fog away and a bright full moon rolled up from behind the mountains which were jeweled with campfires all along the heights to the peak of Lookout. The brightness of the night revealed some of the cost of the day. The Tenth was camped near the field hospital of the Seventeenth Corps, from whose position on the heights where the fighting had been, ambulances and stretcher-bearers began to bring in the wounded and dying. Surgeons worked by torch and candlelight. Taps sounded that night for men who would never fight again, as well as for those snatching a few hours of rest between battles; but Cord could not sleep for the sounds of suffering all around him.

Before daylight, as he drummed reveille, Cord again saw General Sherman, this time in the saddle, riding out to the day's encounter and attended by his staff. As dawn came, men strained to see the flag at the top of Lookout Mountain. Cheer after cheer rose from the camp by the river and wafted up into the hills as the Stars and Stripes showed clearly. A band started to play "The Star-Spangled Banner." Cord, who had waited so long to see and be part of a battle, was now in the thick of one, and if ever a battle could be splendid, that day's was—splendid, and horribly cruel.

At daylight the guns began, their plunging fire pouring down from the hills. Cannon roared until their sound became one continuous roll of thunder, never ceasing, and swallowing mightily all sense of separate concussion. Men in blue pushed up the hillsides and through the ravines, only to discover that the heights so easily taken the day before were not a part of the continuous ridge but a separate hill with an intercepting valley which could be crossed only under raking fire from the enemy's well-placed guns. Yet, blue column after blue column moved forward without faltering until they came to a tunnel out of which enemy troops charged upon them fiercely; then the deadly, close fighting began. Hundreds of lives were lost in shooting and bayoneting and hand-to-hand combat.

Ambulances were rushed into service, horses at the gallop, weaving in and about through the slowly advancing artillery. Farther on, through the smoke and the din, whole divisions were slaughtering each other for the possession of single hills and spurs.

Cord was detailed with Zeb Carson, one of the ambulance drivers, to carry water to the wounded and help the stretcher-bearers. Up and down and over the long battle-strewn way they drove, again and again, from the corps hospitals along the banks of the Chickamauga to the tunnel mouth where men lay as they had fallen on the blood-soaked ground, mangled and torn, the blue and the gray together. They brought down men who were suffering agonies with grim courage and control. Cord stood by while a surgeon examined a big man whose left arm had been shattered by solid shot. It dangled and spurted blood as the soldier tried to hold it in place.

"Can't do anything for you here," the surgeon said as he shook his head gravely. "You'll have to go across the river." He indicated the divisional hospital on the other side of the Tennessee where the worst cases were taken.

The big man seemed to crumple before them.

"That means I'm going to die," he half sobbed. But, after one quivering instant, he straightened himself. Clasping the shattered arm to his side, he looked the surgeon in the eye. "But I'm not going to die." He looked at Cord, then back again at the surgeon and said doggedly, "I tell you, I'm not going to die."

The battle reached its peak of intensity in the early afternoon as two divisions cleared the intercepting valley and flung themselves up the flank of the ridge proper in the face of a storm of cannon fire, musketry and bursting shell. The enemy was concentrating upon them, for new batteries could be seen on the top of the ridge, galloping up, unlimbering, and opening fire. Officers' orders were in vain, since no human voice could be heard above the all-enveloping roar which was presently increased by forty guns of Union artillery in the rear, firing over their own men's heads toward the enemy trenches.

Cord and Zeb Carson were making their way across an opening at the gallop when Zeb pointed down the valley below the ridge toward Orchard Knob. A white line of musketry fire was advancing rapidly, extending farther and farther right and left, and on toward the face of the ridge up which it began to move. Zeb reined in the horses and they watched until the billowy line of white smoke disappeared behind a spur. Presently the firing above them began to lessen. The newly placed Rebel batteries galloped away along the heights as quickly as they had come. Guns grew silent, or turned toward that distant white line of musketry hidden behind the hill but still advancing.

"I'll bet that was Pap Thomas's strike on center," Zeb Carson said, when the lessening fire above them made talk possible. "You see, Pap waited until we'd drawn all the guns out here, then he charged 'em right. Revenge for Chickamauga!"

Cord tugged at his arm and pointed straight up above them where Sherman's men had now scaled the heights amid the greatly diminished firing. In the lull that followed, the sound of musketry at Thomas's center could be plainly heard. Zeb grinned and yelled to his horses. There was no lull for ambulance drivers, nor would there be for long hours to come. It was midnight before news of the quick and glorious capture at sundown of Missionary Ridge by General Thomas's Fourteenth Corps reached the men in camp by the river.

To Cord, that infantry charge straight up the face of the cannon-pierced heights of Missionary Ridge was the most exciting event of his life. Men talked about it around their campfires, adding to its luster with their own experiences. One man told a story of General Grant, watching from his point of observation on Orchard Knob. As he saw the continued advance of the charging regiments which he had expected to stop at the first rifle pits lest they be cut off and destroyed, he became more and more uneasy. "Who ordered those men up the ridge?" he demanded of General Thomas. General Thomas did not know. Turning to General Granger, next in command of the Army of the Cumberland, General Grant asked, "Did you order them up?" "No," was the reply, "but when those fellows get started, all hell can't stop them."

That was the spirit that moved the Army of the Cumberland. Sixty battle flags had led the way with men scrambling after them as hard as they could run, over rocks and broken trees, past fallen comrades, unaware of the rain of shot and shell through which they plunged, forgetting to use their guns in their passion to reach the top of those towering heights toward which they had been gazing for two long days while the battle raged at their right and their left. The rumor that General Grant had thought them unfit for assault had been only an added challenge.

"When the signal came and we got going," a man from the Sixth Indiana said, "we kinda went crazy. The Johnnies must have thought so too, 'cause they started running for their lives before we got to the first rifle pits, and pretty soon we were all tearing up the hill together as if something was after us. Nothing could stop us then. Officers tried to, but gave it up and climbed with us. I was most at the top myself when my captain pulled me back by the coattail. He wanted to get there first. But my wind was better, and I beat him anyway."

"An' you shoulda seen him an' the captain huggin' each other!" another man interrupted. "Everybody was adancin' around there like Indians when I come up—throwin' their haversacks up in the air and yellin' like wild ones. An' gosh, how the Johnnies did skeedaddle down the other side of the mountain! They thought we was possessed."

"I'd a been up as soon as anybody," another chimed in, "if I hadn't been wearing my overcoat. But I counted eleven bullet holes in the old coat when I got to the top, so I guess it was a good job I kept it on."

Men drew diagrams in the earth around their campfires, enclosing a V for the victory which had started on the right with General Hooker and the Army of the Potomac, continued on the left with General Sherman and the Army of the Mississippi, and been completed at center by General Thomas and the Army of the Cumberland. Chattanooga, the impregnable, had been won for the Union.

"Come on, Footey." Zeb was nudging him. "We can't sit around a campfire all night. They's still wounded to be brought in."

It was after midnight and Cord was tired, but the white moon shone down on some twelve thousand men lying dead or in agony among the hills of Chattanooga. The ambulance drivers and their horses, freshened by the brief rest, went back to their tasks. Two hours later Zeb turned to Cord and shook his head sadly.

"I can't drive the old hoss another step, Footey. Where you going to bunk down? Want to sleep with me in the buggy? Crawl in, and I'll be with you in a second." He set about unharnessing his trembling horse.

Cord, too, was trembling with exhaustion. He crept gratefully into the shelter of the ambulance, for the night was cold; he was so quickly asleep that he did not know when Zeb Carson crawled in beside him. He had slept hardly at all for sixty hours, and he had eaten nothing but hardtack.

Less than an hour later, though it might have been an eon so completely had he lost all sense of time, Cord felt himself roughly shaken by the shoulder. Struggling from the depths of the sodden sleep into which he had fallen, he was irritably conscious of Ira Miles pulling and hauling at him, then dragging him forth to stumble along at his side through the moonlit woods by the river. At the reserve camp, the Tenth was already lined up for action. Their brigade had been ordered out in pursuit of the retreating enemy.

Cord shouldered the drum which Old Lacey gave him and fell into step as they set off across the pontoon bridge over the Chickamauga. Through the blurry hours that followed, something inside him and quite beyond his own volition kept him marching on the narrow rutted roads strewn with the debris of retreat, beating the Common Time march with the other drummers, and munching hardtack to stay the emptiness in his stomach. The moon dropped behind the mountain. The sky began to grow light with day. Firing ahead of them was proof that the pursuit was close. But Cord only really came awake when they reached Chickamauga Station.

Here their brigade met with brief but stout resistance, for Chickamauga had been the enemy base of supplies during operations around Chattanooga. A hidden battery opened fire upon them as they emerged on the high ground above the station, but this was soon silenced by their own artillery. The Twenty-first Kentucky Infantry was sent forward to carry the works. A thrill went through the lines at the rear as the battle flags told them that Kentucky Union was now meeting Kentucky Secessionist. A gallant fight ensued, with the enemy finally driven up over the hills beyond and leaving station and storehouses in flames behind them.

The Tenth rushed in upon the fire and wreckage in time to snatch some stores from the burning. They rolled out barrels and carried out boxes and crates amid huge smoking piles of corn meal and corn, broken wagons, abandoned caissons, pontoon fragments, and all the half-ruined accumulation and salvage of a projected advance northward. Some of the corn meal was undamaged and they fell hungrily upon it, devouring it by the fistful. DeGraff, the bass drummer, not so fat as he used to be, found a treat for them when he knocked in the top of a barrel of molasses and began to scoop up handfuls of the brown liquid. With whoops of joy, others found barrels of their own and it became a wild frolic. They had had no sweets for many weeks, not even sugar for their coffee.

Bending over a barrel and scooping ravenously, more than one fellow was tripped up by the heels and plunged in head first, to be hauled forth dripping by his mates. Then they swarmed about him, yelling and laughing, as they took the more convenient way of scooping their molasses off him rather than from the barrel. Before the frolic was stopped by an angry officer, one of the men had been tipped into a barrel of soft soap and sopped greedily until the mistake was discovered amid sputtering and coughing, swearing and weeping, as the strong stuff nearly strangled him.

The feeling that they were on the road to victory and the good fill of food gave Cord a new strength. He marched and drummed with the others, forgetting his fatigue though he sorely missed his haversack which had been left behind under Zeb Carson's ambulance and by now was lost forever. Two days and two nights of pursuing the enemy brought them near Ringgold in Georgia where General Sherman had established temporary headquarters. He gave them their orders briefly. They were to turn back to Knoxville to head off possible enemy reinforcements.

The Tenth had been marching on battle rations. The memory of the food stores they had devoured at Chickamauga was all they had to give variety to hardtack and water. As the men with whom Cord was marching ascended an embankment in open formation, Cord stumbled over the body of an enemy soldier lying in a ditch. A few months ago he might have been shocked at the sight. Now all he was aware of was that the fallen soldier had a very good haversack for which he would have no more use. Cord needed a haversack badly, so he knelt down beside the mangled body, cut the straps of the haversack with his knife, and adjusted them to fit over his own shoulders. Before putting it on he looked in to see what it might contain. Inside he found only three partly gnawed corncobs.

The Johnnies are hungrier than we are, he thought as he swung the haversack over his shoulder and scrambled up the embankment after the others.

General Sherman was waiting for them at Charleston, thirty miles north, when they reached there two days later. Two other divisions, coming in over different roads, arrived with the Tenth. They were weary and footsore, half-starved, and nearly frozen, for they had marched five days on two days' rations. Most of them were without overcoats or blankets, which had been left behind at White House Landing when they had stripped for action at Missionary Ridge. But the taste of victory was still theirs and the elation carried them on. The drums beat bravely, especially the drummer boy of Company F, as if to convey support to one of their number.

Old Lacey had given out completely toward the end of the march. A wagon had been found for him and he had been taken directly to the field hospital at Charleston. Cord,

George Jay, Ira Miles, and all the rest of the Drum Corps had put a spirit they were far from feeling into their drumming as they swung the Tenth into Charleston. They did it for their drum major, hoping that somehow he would know. Later that night when they tried to get some information about Pop's condition, Captain Hart shook his head gravely and said they might not know for a few days but that it was doubtful that Old Lacey would march with them again.

"He's not going to die, is he?" George Jay asked in a hoarse voice.

The captain smiled at the boy's anxiety and said consolingly, "No, but he may have to be invalided home."

Knoxville was now on the lips of all, for rumor had it that General Burnside's army was besieged there and at the verge of surrender, for the town was surrounded by enemy forces in greatly superior number. And rumor was confirmed that night in General Sherman's message to the men in camp. It was a warmly friendly message of congratulation to them upon their soldierly achievement in the recent battles, and of sympathy for the hardship so cheerfully endured in the marches of pursuit.

"But now, my comrades in arms," the message concluded, "a vastly greater effort is demanded of you. Twelve thousand of our fellow soldiers are beleaguered in the mountain town of Knoxville, who must have relief within three days. We will move to their support at daylight, tomorrow."

"Three cheers for Old Cump!" someone shouted.

The men hurrahed and hurrahed.

The drummers were out before dawn, led by Ira Miles. They put a zest into reveille and then into the General Assembly that brought the men from their tents and onto the parade ground ready for action. Rations were issued, each man receiving three crackers, three teaspoonfuls of coffee beans, a half teaspoonful of sugar, a half pint of beans, and a chunk of fat bacon, with orders to make it go as far as possible. The drums began on the Long March and the men turned by companies off the parade ground and onto the road.

They knew that before them lay a forced march of nearly eighty miles which might well be the peak of effort and hardship in their war experience, but there was not a man who was not ready for it. Eagerness might have carried them ahead too fast, but the drummers as usual set the pace and marching steps fell into it. Pop Lacey, standing by a field hospital tent, had watched them as they went off. He was bitterly disappointed that he could not be with the Tenth on their long march, but he was proud of the men he had trained and he knew they could measure up. Cord and George had turned away when they saw him standing there with tears in his eyes, saving to put into their drumming the words they could not say.

Cord set out with the zest of a crusader. His brother George was with General Burnside, as were dozens of the boys from home. He was filled with an aching, urgent desire to see them as he thought about them, and a terrible fear that they might not get there in time. As he trudged over the hard rough road he found himself picturing the heroic rescue of them all by himself and his friends of the Tenth.

But presently he was just pushing along as before, with no thought save of the cruel hardness of the roads through paper-thin soles. He knew he was lucky to have any soles at all, for he had seen men barefoot that morning, tearing strips from their blankets to wrap around their feet in place of shoes. It was cold, with a raw east wind in their faces. They ate acorns as they marched, or gnawed corncobs with which they had filled their haversacks before they set out. They marched twenty miles before nightfall, and the next day by a terrible effort they made nineteen miles, pushing on for two hours after dark.

Cord's heart sank when he learned that they were still a good forty miles from Knoxville, for three days was the time during which it had been said relief must come; and they could never make forty miles in another day.

By midafternoon of the third day they had marched fourteen miles when they found themselves halted by the Little Tennessee River spread wide before them opposite Morganton, where the enemy had destroyed two bridges and run a locomotive and a long train of cars into the river. Scouts and pioneers searched in vain for a possible crossing, but the river was more than two hundred yards wide, never less than five feet deep in mid-channel, and the water was bitterly cold. There was nothing for it but the engineers.

As the men waited for a bridge to be constructed, some seized the chance to go foraging; but Cord would not leave the riverbank. Hour after hour he watched as the engineers crossed the river by raft and began to build the bridge, using cribwork and trestles and planking from deserted and partly burned houses in Morganton. As the afternoon waned and the bridge grew foot by foot, Cord wondered desperately what was happening in Knoxville. Captain Beach said that he thought the cavalry had certainly got through to the rescue, but Cord found small comfort in the conjecture.

When a foraging party returned with a cow, Cord ceased watching the engineers and gave his attention to the butchering. It occurred to him that the tallow of the entrails would be good to fry his allotment of beef in, but as he walked away with a portion of it in his skillet he was suddenly seized with an irresistible desire for something in his empty stomach. He began to gulp down the raw tallow, and kept on gulping it ravenously until every bit of it was gone. Then he lay down on the hard ground in a patch of pale sunshine and fell asleep.

A long time afterward, as it seemed to Cord, Ira Miles waked him up to eat a huge chunk of beef that he had roasted for Cord. Few things had ever tasted so good. For some men it was the first fresh beef they had eaten since leaving home, nearly two years ago.

At four o'clock in the morning, the regiments began to move cautiously across the improvised bridge which the engineers had just completed. Company F of the Tenth was hardly over when the bridge broke, and they were compelled to wait for repairs to be made before the rest of the regiment could join them safely. There were other delays, and nightfall found them only five miles farther on their way toward Knoxville, still bravely hoping to reach their goal by another day's marching.

The next day they pushed on through drenching rain, buoyed by the driving incentive of emergency. Near Maryville an orderly galloped up to them with news, and orders. General Burnside had defeated General Longstreet and all was well with the Union forces. The Fourteenth Corps was not needed in Knoxville and was to turn back to Chattanooga.

The men cheered with one breath and groaned with the next. Ira Miles said that it was a hard thing when good news could be disappointing. With no great goal in sight, the men realized that they were tired, hungry, and cold. Cord, shivering in his wet clothes, felt just then that he would rather die than march back to Chattanooga.

But march back they did.

On the way they were delayed again and again by slashing winter rains, between which there were times of freezing cold. Foraging was difficult and scanty. They lived mainly on parched corn, which they stayed up nights to prepare when the weather allowed, and then ate on the march. When an occasional cow was brought in for butchering, the hide was eagerly seized upon for cowhide boots, as they called the crude moccasins made from the cowskin, wearing the hair next to their bare feet for warmth. Bill Foster killed a coon and made moccasins of coonskin for himself and Cord which were the envy of the regiment.

Three weeks from the time they were turned back at Maryville, at dusk of a bitter evening with a knifelike gale blowing, they reached the site of the pontoon bridge by which they had crossed to the battle of Missionary Ridge; but the bridge had been swept away by heavy rains. Weary, ragged, hungry, they felt as if they could endure no more. Then loud halloos of welcome greeted them from the camp across the river.

"Get along to the ferry," Wardie Fisher called. "I've got grub for you."

Two hours later found them seven miles downriver, waiting near Chattanooga at a bend in the river where a swing ferry could carry them across. This was a large and clumsy scow hitched to the end of a cable, the other end of which was wrapped around a tree a few hundred yards beyond, at the head of the bend. By manipulating the slab of wood that served as rudder, the current was made to carry the big boat back and forth on a long diagonal across the broad sweep of the river. It was a tedious process at best, and the rising gale made passage more difficult than usual, and extremely dangerous. Each crossing took an hour, and a load was hardly a hundred men.

Company F of the Tenth awaited its turn, huddled in the shelter of a row of brick buildings which broke the biting sweep of the gale as it tore down the river. When they could stand the cold no longer, they ripped the tar roofing from the buildings and burned it. But the coldest hour of all came when they were packed in the ferry too close to stir, with blown water spraying over them and the wind cutting through them as it shrilled by. Reaching the other side, they climbed out stiffly; but seven miles' march soon limbered them.

The regiment became a disorganized mob as the men pushed into the wind, doggedly, silently. When the men in the lead could get the wind from the camp at White House Landing, they began to run.

"Coffee!" they yelled, as they raced toward camp.

Others plunged over the hill after them to the fires that gleamed ahead. A last panting thrust was made, five hundred yards of charging, stumbling effort, and the leaders were in camp, soon to be joined by the rest of the men. They stabbed their bayonets into the ground, hung up their accouterments, grabbed their tin dishes, and staggered toward the fire where a huge kettle of coffee, cauldrons of baked beans and piles of johnnycake awaited them. Wardie and the camp guards had been foraging for weeks to gather the feast they now offered.

Squatted on the ground about the fires, in the shelter of the windbreak of tall trees, men ate and ate until their stomachs would take no more. Groaning, they stretched themselves on the ground and slept.

The Tennessee campaign was over.

CHAPTER IX

No REVEILLE WAS SOUNDED for the Tenth the morning after their return to White House Landing. When the men began to stir in the late morning, the wind had spent itself and the sun shone warm and bright. By common consent, it was cleanup day. Men had not washed or shaved for more than a month and they were a grizzly lot. Stripping themselves of their tattered remnants of clothing, they put the verminous rags to boil in huge kettles of brine—Wardie's bean kettles— or their own coffeepots. The hardiest of the men bathed in the icy waters of the Tennessee, and the rest scrubbed each other by the fires. Barbering and shaving went on while the clothes dried. A few thrifty ones tried to mend their tatters before dressing again, but the majority donned their uniforms contentedly, awaiting the promised issue of new ones.

A few days later, the entire brigade went into winter quarters at Chickamauga, seven miles below Chattanooga. They lived in log cabins, each cabin six feet square, with bunks across one end and a fireplace opening at the other into a chimney built outside. The roofs were covered with the heavy cloth of their shelter tents, which served well in a winter of icy winds and little snow. Cord shared a cabin with Ira Miles, who had been advanced to drum major now that Old Lacey had been invalided home, George Jay, and a new drummer named John Jennings who had taken Ira's place in the ranks.

When George made the mistake of calling the new recruit Johnny, the boy had turned to him with angry eyes, "Call me Jennie, or anything else you like," he said. "I won't be a Johnny as long as we're fighting Johnny Rebs."

So Jennie he was, and a good friend he became to Cord, for he was nearer Cord's age than anyone else in the Drum Corps.

On Christmas day, the boys were ready to do anything to have a treat, for they were still on quarter rations and Wardie Fisher's feast of welcome was a fading memory. Foraging was forbidden. Jennie brought in a sack of shelled corn, mules' feed which he picked up on a visit to the corrals, and Ira Miles saw possibilities in it. He showed the boys how to hull it. First he put it to boil in a kettle with ashes which removed the hull, then he ran it through several vessels of water to take the lye out of the kernels. Cord's share in the work was to walk half a mile in the wind every time a fresh pail of water was needed. They kept at their hulling the whole of a bleak and blustery day, and ate hulled corn until they were ready to burst.

Life in the camp was comfortable despite the quarter rations, and leisure was welcome after the strenuous campaign months. They played cards endlessly and read dime novels by the dozen, for there seemed an unlimited supply. Once a week or so a brace of fiddlers got together and sponsored a gander dance, at which the soldiers taught each other to waltz, tying handkerchiefs on the arms of the men who were to be girls.

The only military duty was roll call, morning and evening, and an occasional brigade drill. On these, Cord was always detailed as a marker and carried the flag to a point a mile in advance for the brigade to march to and form a new battle line. It was tedious standing there sometimes more than an hour, waiting for the brigade to come up, and one day he had the bright idea of carrying a dime novel that had been sent him from home in his pocket to help pass the time. For a drill or two, the diversion passed unnoticed. Reading away one morning, with his right hand on the flagstaff and his left hand holding the book, he became so spellbound by a Wild West tale of threatened massacre that he was wholly unconscious of Brigadier General Morgan who had ridden up and was watching him disapprovingly.

"Young man, have you forgotten that you are on duty? Don't you know enough to salute your general?"

In his confusion Cord almost dropped the flag as he tried to pocket the thrilling volume.

"What's the story?" the general asked. He took the book from Cord's reluctant hand and turned through it slowly.

Cord stood beside him, still rigid with the suspense of the story. He watched with bated breath until the general presently gave it back to him with an amiable twinkle in his eyes.

"Heaven only knows why you boys want to read that trash," he said, "but if you must, see that you confine your reading to camp. Get along now, young man, and remember you're a marker for a civilized brigade, and not an Indian scout."

"Yes, sir," Cord replied as he saluted smartly, but he wondered how he would ever control his suspense through two more hours of drill and until after roll call that evening.

Camp life had not begun to pall when government agents

arrived from Washington proposing re-enlistment for three years. They promised higher pay, new uniforms, and an immediate thirty-day furlough. Out of the nearly six hundred members that the Michigan Tenth now numbered, all but thirty-five enlisted for veteran service. It was no fault of Cord's that he was counted among the thirty-five. He had presented himself for re-enlistment as eagerly as any of the men when they were marched past the mustering officers, single file, a company at a time.

"Can't take you, my boy." An officer drew him out of the line. "You're too small."

Lieutenant Colonel Dickerson tried to intervene. "He's been with us from the first, Officer. Done good service, too."

Cord smiled up at the colonel in gratitude.

"Can't help it," said the officer brusquely, "he's too small. My orders are very strict. Clear out, young'un."

The long line moved on to the mustering office without Cord. It was a dark disappointment, and the eager furlough plans he heard all about him did not lighten it.

Later that day, Lieutenant Colonel Dickerson called him into his office. "I did everything I knew how to convince them, Cordie, but it was no use. You're to finish your three years that began when you enlisted in January '62, but they'll not grant you a veteran enlistment. However, I'm bound I'll get you a furlough permit, whether or no. I've seen General Thomas about it."

This was cheering news, and Cord began to make his plans as the other men were making theirs. Perhaps the war would be over before his enlistment was up. As for being a veteran, he felt like one whatever the mustering officer had to say. He knew now what war was, and if that didn't constitute a veteran no words on paper could make any difference.

Three weeks went by. Furlough papers came for the others, but none for Cord. Only two days remained before the men were scheduled to start back to Michigan. The thirty-five who would be left behind were to be regimented with the Tenth Illinois. Cord received orders to move to another cabin. Bill Foster dropped in that morning to commiserate with him, but Cord was too glum for conversation. He was wondering how he could endure to see the others start off without him.

"Say, Footey," said Bill, after vain attempts to cheer Cord, "what do you say to a prowl up the ridge? I'd like to get some laurel root to take home with me."

It was a better way to spend the day, Cord decided, than to sit around camp and hear all his friends talking about going home. So he and Bill Foster set off together toward the bronzed bare heights of Missionary Ridge.

They tramped on and on through the woods and the zest of the clear winter day began to fill them with new energy. By early afternoon they had climbed to the top of the ridge and Bill had found all the laurel he could carry. Digging about for a last bit, Bill dislodged a big stone. They watched it go bounding down the long, rugged slope until it caught in the crotch of a tree a half mile below them. That set them off. For two hours they pried loose the biggest stones they could find, sometimes boulders taller than themselves, and sent them crashing down the mountainside.

Time had gone by without their knowing it and they got back to camp late for roll call. Ordered to appear before the judge advocate, he sentenced them to solitary confinement for the night.

"Mighty heavy payment for a few hours' sport," grumbled Bill Foster, who was used to paying for good times.

Cord wondered why their offense warranted such serious punishment. The next day they found out.

During their absence, the brigade had been ordered out to Ringgold. The Michigan Tenth had been sharply engaged by the enemy just over the Georgia line in the shadow of a rocky height which towered above a range known as Rocky Face Ridge. In the stony wilderness they had lost sixty men by surprise attack, among them Lieutenant Colonel Dickerson who was in command of the regiment.

The Nashville and Chattanooga papers which were brought into camp that night carried dramatic accounts of the attack. Cord, knowing he might have been in it himself, had to content himself with reading about it.

> With their furloughs in their pockets [Cord read] and preparations made to visit their dear ones at home from whom they had been parted so long, yesterday's bugles found the Michigan Tenth put to an unusual test of patriotism, and bravely responsive, with flags unfurled, and on the march to the field of battle. Under General Morgan at Buzzard's Roost, they fought with the Sixtieth Illinois beneath the shadows of towering Rocky Face Ridge, carrying the colors to the enemy's very works through a murderous fire of infantry and artillery. They gallantly advanced over two sharp ridges, and when preparing to ascend the third, were checked by a raking enfilading fire of canister, shot from the right and left, which tore relentlessly and fatally along the entire line, adding to the terrible musketry fire from the swarming host on the Ridge, and was fearfully destructive to human life. The Tenth was terribly cut up, losing some sixty men in a very few minutes, and Lieutenant Colonel Dickerson, commanding, is wounded and a prisoner in the hands of the enemy.

Cord's disappointment at not getting a furlough seemed small in the shadow of this blow to the regiment. They had lost hardly twelve men in encounter in the two years preceding, and now a tenth of their number were killed, wounded, or taken prisoner in a single action. And on the eve of furlough! Indeed, it was after furlough officially had begun. For two days the furloughed men waited, hoping for an exchange of prisoners, but it could not be arranged. Sixteen men of the Tenth, including their beloved commander, were sent to Andersonville Prison for the remainder of the war. Home-going was deeply shadowed by the unexpected tragedy in the ranks of the Michigan Tenth.

On the morning of March 12, 1864, Cord watched his comrades leave for their homes, and Michigan. He admired their new uniforms and the way they marched, and his heart ached to be going along with them; but he stoically set about moving into his new quarters with the Tenth Illinois. He had hardly got there when an orderly rode into camp, bringing furlough papers from General Thomas for Coridon E. Foote, drummer boy of Company F, Tenth Michigan Infantry.

"That's me!" Cord shouted.

With a whoop of joy, he threw his few possessions into his haversack, shouted his good-bys, and was off on the road to Chattanooga at his best marching gait. It was three o'clock in the afternoon, only a few hours since the other furloughed men had left, and Cord felt that he had a good chance of catching up with them.

Arriving in Chattanooga just before dark, Cord went straight to the station, only to find that a train had left for the north within the hour and that there would not be another until the next morning. His friends were on their way and it was likely now that they would get to Michigan before he did. Cord then headed for the railroad yards, hunting through the tangle of tracks until he found a locomotive with steam up which was bound for Nashville with a long train of freight cars. He walked beside it until he found an empty with a door he could open. Climbing aboard, he spread his blanket on the floor in a corner and lay down to sleep.

At Stevenson he was wakened by an officer with a lantern who stood in the open door of the car. "Who are you, young man, and where are you bound?"

Cord handed him his furlough papers.

The officer checked them carefully. "All right, sonny, you're no deserter. Run home to your ma, and have a good time."

Cord was wakened again when it began to rain. Streams of icy water poured in on him through the ventilator as the train ran through the steep railway cuts that lay along the way. Move where he would about the car, there seemed no escaping the water. But morning came at last, bright and clear. When the train slowed down for a station, Cord climbed to the top of the car, spread out his blanket, and lay down beside it to dry. As far as he could determine, he was the only passenger on a train that was at least half a mile long. The thought made him feel lonely, and he determined that the next time they slowed for a station he would walk along the top of the cars and find the train crew.

"An' look at the drowned rat what's washed in on us last night!" the fireman announced Cord to the engineer.

"Drowned rat, your granny," answered the engineer as he looked Cord over in a fatherly way. "Can't you see he's a poor drummer lad from the front? Move along, Tim, an' give him a place by your fire."

They asked Cord endless questions and enjoyed his account of life at the front. At the next station they stopped for breakfast and Cord was invited to join them. The rough bench and counter of the railway shanty were unaccustomed luxury to Cord, for he had not sat down to a table to eat in a very long time. The ham and eggs, pancakes, coffee, bread and butter which were set before him tasted like something from another world. When he had cleaned up his plate in an unbelievably short time, the engineer, immensely pleased, ordered a second serving for him, and then a third. Cord looked at the third longingly, but he could not compass it.

Leaving his new-found friends in the railroad yards at

Nashville, he spent two nights at the Zollicopher House while awaiting transportation north. When he got it, it was the luxury of a passenger train to Louisville, where he again spent the night in a Soldiers' Home. Next morning in the pouring rain, he crossed the Ohio by ferry and took a freight train to Indianapolis. En route, the rain turned to snow and he reached Indianapolis nearly frozen, long after dark, in the thick of a bitter, blinding storm.

It was Saturday night and he was told at the station that there would be no more trains until Monday morning. A kindly policeman offered to start him on his way to the Soldiers' Home, which was on the other side of the city. He walked with Cord through the storm to the end of his beat, where another policeman took charge of him, and then another, who finally pointed out to him the lights of the Home. They showed blurrily through the whirling snow just beyond a broad common and Cord staggered toward them through the drifts. When the door opened to him at last, no place in the world had ever seemed so warm and inviting.

There were three big stoves with roaring fires around which clustered soldiers. Some had fiddles and harmonicas and were making music, some were playing cards. A group of good folk of the town served coffee and sandwiches during the evening. There were straw-covered bunks in tiers around the big room, but Cord preferred a space on the floor between two stoves for sleeping.

There he spent Sunday, soaking up heat. Monday morning he caught a train to Toledo. That night he and two other Michigan soldiers slept under a table in the railway station in order to be on hand for the five o'clock train to Detroit in the morning. One more night was spent in the Soldiers' Home at Detroit, but Cord was so excited he could hardly close his eyes. A train ride to Fentonville in the morning brought him to the last lap of his journey which was made by stagecoach from Fentonville to Flint.

The day was warm and sunny. The snow was nearly all gone and the road was very muddy. Cord was the only passenger. He sat on the high seat in front beside the driver, who plied him with questions about life at the front; but as the old landmarks began to appear and Cord realized that he was nearly home, he no more heard the driver's questions than he could have answered them just then. They drew up with a flourish before the Carleton House, the chief hotel in the town. Sid Rosevelt, the son of the proprietor, came down the steps to greet them in the customary manner. When he saw who was arriving, he took Cord's hand in his and shook it.

"How'do, Foote, how'do. Always a privilege to welcome one of our brave fellows from the front."

Cord wanted to say something, but could find no words.

Sid's eyes took in the ragged cotton shirt, only partially concealed by the blanket Cord wore on his shoulders, the soiled and baggy trousers hitched high because they were so much too large, and finally the worn-out shoes.

"Good Lord, you look tough! Don't they give you anything to wear?"

Cord grinned his embarrassment, and set off along Saginaw Street toward his father's harness shop. He had not gone far when he came upon some of his former schoolmates playing marbles on the sidewalk. First they stared at him, then they set up a shout of welcome.

"Gosh, it's Cordie Foote, home from the war! Hey, fellows—" and the cry went out to other groups across the street.

They swarmed around him and walked along with him to his father's shop. Cord felt strangely tongue-tied among them, and was glad they did not follow him inside. As the little bell gave its familiar tinkle when the shop door opened, and then again when the door closed behind him, Cord felt as if his heart was standing still.

"Hello—" he called in a voice he hardly knew was his own.

Instead of his father coming out to meet him from the workroom at the rear, it was Ward, the old man who helped his father. He wore his spectacles perched high on his forehead. Seeing someone standing near the door, he hauled them down to peer through them.

"Wh-wh-why, C-C-Cordie F-F-Foote," he stuttered, as he always did when surprised. "Is it you?" he asked unbelievingly. "How you've grown, boy! How you've grown!"

Cord grinned. No words could have pleased him more.

The old hands patted his shoulders and felt his arms, but the eyes seemed unable to do anything but stare at him. "Your pappy'll be glad to see you, Cordie," he said at last. "You'll be a ton-tonic for him. You see, he—he had a stroke day before yesterday and he's a perty sick man, Cordie. You run right along home now, my boy, and let him see you. It's g-g-good you came."

Old Ward tried to send him out the front door, but Cord knew the boys were waiting there. He followed Ward to the workroom, all the while asking questions about his father, then he slipped out the back door and up the alley, hoping no one else would see him before he reached home. He felt strange and foreign, and almost afraid to see his father.

When he came to the house, a few blocks farther on, he could not get himself to go up the front steps. Instead, he went around to the back door and knocked. No one answered. He knocked again more firmly, and then opened the door.

His mother was in the kitchen, hurrying toward the door. She stopped, and her eyes grew startled. Then she shrieked aloud and began to cry. For a moment Cord wished that he were back in winter quarters at Chattanooga.

"It's just me, Ma." He went up to her shyly.

She put an arm around him, but kept on helplessly crying.

A neighbor came out through the pantry. "Land sakes, Mrs. Foote, what can the matter be?"

At a glance she took in the situation—Mrs. Foote's tears and Cord's expression of dismay. "Why, it's Cordie come home from the war! Never mind your ma's crying, Cordie. She's just tuckered out. She'll be all right in a minute."

Soon his mother's sobbing quieted and she was able to tell Cord that one of the men of his regiment had only just gone out the front door. "He's been with me in the parlor the last hour, telling me about the brave and terrible things you boys have been doing, and how you couldn't re-enlist or come home on furlough. I was crying about you then, and trying to think how I'd ever tell your poor father, when I walked right into you in the kitchen. Oh, Cordie, don't you even have a coat to wear?" She began to cry again. "But what a man you are!"

That night his father was better, enough better to listen eagerly to Cord's account of his adventures. On Sunday, two days later, all the neighbors were asked in while Cord told his story again, and in greater detail. He was fed and feted and called on. His mother made him two new uniforms—a plain one, and a Zouave to dress up in.

During his twenty-six days of furlough, Cord never felt quite at home with anyone except Old Lacey.

"Gosh, Pop, the rest of 'em can't imagine what it's like down there," he said one day, toward the last of his furlough. "No use tryin' to tell 'em, either."

"Not much, Cordie," Old Lacey answered a little sadly.

"Not much, because most of 'em think they know such a goldern lot more about it than we do!"

On April 12th furlough officially ended, and the men of the Tenth gathered at the old barracks from which they had set out in the beginning and where they had drilled in those long-ago days before they knew anything about actual war. But it was not until the 20th that orders came to them to return to the front. It was all very much as in April two years before, but there was no feasting this time in Holly. War was no longer an exhilarating adventure to be entered upon in holiday mood, but rather a grim business to be got through with as quickly and expeditiously as possible.

Five days later they reached Nashville and spent the night on the old Cherry Creek campground. In the morning they drew rations and ammunition and set forth on the road to Stone's River, feeling themselves veterans indeed as they passed the familiar landmarks of early struggle. The country was lush with the beauty and sweet with the fragrance of southern springtime. They made a record march of twenty-five miles to Murfreesboro.

It was the first of May, and very hot in the sun, when they marched into Shelbyville one afternoon a few days later and stopped for an hour's rest in the tree-shaded square around which the little town was built. Cord stretched on his back on a sloping cellar door in the shade of a house by the roadside. He had almost dropped asleep when he heard an alarm and looked up. Far out along the straight white road they were about to follow, a great cloud of dust was coming toward them. Officers hurried to examine it with their glasses. Everywhere men roused themselves for action. Enemy cavalry were known to be making bold raids northward. Blue uniforms, not gray, came within view of the officers' glasses, and the men soon dropped back to positions of ease.

Some were asleep again by the time the cavalry brigade

came clattering into town, with clanking sabers and creaking saddles, mingled with a strong odor of leather and hard-ridden horseflesh. Cord sat up on his cellar door to watch them go by. The cavalry was still his secret admiration, and these men in their trim blue uniforms, however dust-covered, were a brave sight. Suddenly a rider spurred out of the ranks and up to where Cord sat alone on his small elevation by the roadside.

"By gosh, Cordie Foote! What are you doing here?" It was Charlie Summers, a chum of Cord's brother George, who had enlisted with his college regiment, the Fourth Michigan Cavalry.

In a moment he was joined by another cavalryman. "Hello, Cord Foote! Where'd you come from?"

It was George Miles, who lived scarcely a block away at home, and whose mother had been in to see Cord many times during furlough. Then Dr. Fish's son, Jim, came up, and Andrew Ward and Charlie, Old Ward's boys, and several others from Flint.

"Good Lord, Cordie Foote, how did you get into the army?"

"Easy." Cord grinned back at them, scrambling to his feet with delight. "I'm drummer for Company F, Tenth Michigan Infantry, First Brigade, Second Division, Fourteenth Corps, Army of the Cumberland. And," he finished as he saluted smartly, "you know Pap Thomas's Army of the Cumberland!"

"Hear! Hear!"

When they heard that he was just back from furlough, they hurled questions at him about his brother George and clamored for news from home; but before he could answer half their questions an officer rode up.

"Have to move along, men. You're blocking the highway. No time for reunions."

"Tell George that you saw us, Cordie," they said as they wheeled their horses around and spurred away.

"I'll tell him you ride better 'n Morgan's Raiders," Cord called after them.

Soon the famous Fourth had gone, in a cloud of dust as they had come, and the town square drowsed again in the May sunshine. Cord almost felt that he must have dreamed the encounter, but real in his hand was a paper cone filled with wild strawberries which one of the cavalrymen had given him. He sat down to eat them as George Jay came along.

"Gosh, Cord, the cavalry's slick!"

"You always did have a hankerin' to ride a hoss, didn't you, Georgie? Me, I'd rather drive a mule." Cord grinned and offered George his pick from the paper cone of berries.

Day after day of steady marching followed, with dust and heat increasing—Tullahoma, Decherd, Tantallon, Stevenson. It was terribly hot at Stevenson. At Bridgeport, the next night, they camped on the island and enjoyed a swim in the Tennessee. Two nights later, at the close of a sultry day, they camped at the foot of Lookout Mountain on a grassy slope beside the river. In the night there was a sudden storm, with a high wind that blew their tents down, and a deluge of water from the mountainside which all but washed them into the river. They arrived at the old winter quarters on the 12th of May, just two months after starting northward on furlough. Orders awaited them to proceed at once and join the brigade for action near Resaca, Georgia.

The next day was hot and the roads were hard going after the heavy rain, but they went out of their way to visit the scene of the battle of Buzzard's Roost. Cord and Bill Foster spent the time there climbing about with George Jay, who gave them a vivid picture of the bloody action they had missed by their laurel-root expedition. They were about to drop down for some rest in a cool and shady ravine when Cord saw a board with a rude inscription on it, tilted above a row of mounds which were evidently recent graves. Bill was already stretched on the mossy ground, half asleep, but George came to stand beside Cord and read the crude lettering:

8 YANKEES GONE TO HEAVEN I HOPE—
WHERE THERE IS NO FIGHTING AND WHERE GOD
JUDGES WHO IS RIGHT OR WRONG

"Gosh, Cord, there's some of our boys lyin' there."

Distantly they heard the bugle through the noontime stillness, calling them to duty. The sound echoed and re-echoed from Rocky Face to Buzzard's Roost as the Tenth roused itself to march on for the spring campaign in Georgia.

CHAPTER X

THE SPRING AND SUMMER campaign in Georgia developed into a gigantic fencing bout between two skilled commanders —Sherman and Johnston—with vast armies for their weapons of thrust and parry, quick eluding, and sudden resistance. For a long time both generals evaded direct attack by feinting, flanking, decoying, retreating. For their men it became a process of marching, sniping, dodging, digging in. General Sherman called it "big Indian war."

The Confederate General Johnston hoped to lure the larger Union army as far as possible from its base of supplies; then a quick blow and the cutting of lines of communication might wipe it out completely. He began a series of retreats, with skillful traps arranged for his pursuers. But General Sherman eluded the traps by flanking rather than directly pursuing the enemy; more than once he compelled a retreat begun by intention to continue from necessity. His immediate care was not so much that of defeating the Southern army, by which he would inflict only a flesh wound upon the enemy cause, as it was to accomplish the fatal damaging of the rich country above and about the city of Atlanta, on which the Confederacy depended largely for both mineral and agricultural supplies. Such a wound would cut through the very heart of the enemy and bring the war to a speedy close. Wanton destruction, it would be called; it was, rather, purposeful destruction of men's property with the ultimate object of saving men's lives.

Soldiers in the ranks knew only vaguely of these larger issues. But, as the campaign proceeded, however much they might be shifted about in burning sun and torrential rain, they had always a sense of intelligent direction and definite objective. Gone were the days of wearisome waiting and timid experimenting. They were engaged now in action and achievement.

"Uncle Billy knows what he's about," the men said, grumbling less and sometimes not at all as they carried out their orders.

For the Tenth, the campaign began with a thirty-mile march to Rome, Georgia, as part of a vast flanking movement. When they set forth at daybreak, the day after they had joined their brigade at Resaca, the May morning was gay with bird song and bloom. The drummers rolled out the calls with zest. It was not long before the sun was blazing above them with a torrid intensity that silenced all bird song and made even drumming difficult. The six-inch dust of the road, stirred up by marching feet, enveloped the men in gritty, choking clouds. Water was scarce. Canteens once emptied could not be refilled for long, hot miles. Men gasped and cried for water as they pushed along. Some dropped by the wayside to await the cool of the day. Many more lagged behind. The footsore vanguard, comprising about half the regiment, reached a camping place near Rome at nine in the evening, after what had been the longest march of their war experience. Stragglers kept coming in all night.

Cord was one of the six of the eighteen drummers who kept his place during the day. There were blisters the size of silver dollars on the soles of his aching feet. His lips were parched and his tongue swollen from thirst; his body throbbed with exhaustion. While Ira and George and Jennie set up camp and started to fry the bacon, Cord's task was to find the nearest creek and fill their canteens. He came upon one after a half hour's searching. First he filled their tin water bucket, then the string of canteens. Tired and aching as he was, he could not resist the temptation to sit down in the swirling water with his clothes on, just to feel its swift coolness wash around him and sweep some of the deadly weariness away. When he returned to camp wet and dripping, the boys thought he had fallen in; and Cord was tired enough to let them think so. Without saying a word, he peeled off his clothes and hung them by the fire to dry.

Their life was one of grueling effort, day after day. But whatever their hardship, it was always visibly shared by the general commanding, whose slouch-hatted, red-bearded figure was a fiery directing presence at every turn. Around their campfires at night, men matched stories of General Sherman, familiarly calling him "Uncle Billy" or "Old Cump"; some of the stories were legend, others were of direct personal encounters. A private in an eastern corps liked to relate how one morning, early in the campaign, he had passed a red-bearded man lying coatless, sleeping against a tree, with his vest unbuttoned and his feet sprawled out before him.

"Is that a general?" he had asked an orderly who was standing near. Upon being told that it was, he exploded with wrath. "A fine way we're commanded, with our generals lying drunk beside the road!"

Quick as a flash, General Sherman had sprung to his feet.

"Stop, my man," he said, "I'm not drunk! While you were sleeping last night, I was planning for you, sir. Now I was taking a nap."

On every hand, as the days went by, there was unmistakable evidence of his planning. Most impressive was the certainty with which rations came through as they were needed, though at times they were only corn meal and bacon. Mail began to be delivered with comforting frequency, no matter what wilderness they might be camped in. The men knew later that this had been accomplished by General Sherman's commandeering of the railroads, forbidding their use for civilian traffic. He was, by this means, able to obtain the stupendous total of one hundred and twenty ten-ton carloads of supplies at his advance base each day. No soldier ever marched without carrying three days' rations; a twenty days' reserve was kept in the regimental wagons to ensure against blocking of the railroad.

Another evidence of careful planning was the presence of mappers and topographical engineers who preceded every advance, charting and photographing the terrain, then rushing their plates and drawings to "dark wagons" which accompanied them, and speedily providing the officers with needed knowledge of the country ahead. There were field telegraphers, too, with light wagons always close to the front. From these they strung wires and insulators to the trees so that a general might keep in communication with his subordinates. Some of the operators were so expert that when separated from their instruments they could by cutting the wires receive a message with their tongues.

Pontoniers had become equally expert and available. Every unit of advance was accompanied by a wagon train loaded with boatlike frames which, at need, could be quickly slid into their canvas cases, dropped from wagons to water, strung together with cables and guy ropes, planked with boards, and so provide a bridge for the waiting army.

The effect of such provision and preparation was not only inspiring to the men who marched with Sherman, it was depressing to the enemy. A group of prisoners one day stood watching the pontoniers at work deftly fitting the canvas to the skeleton boat frames. "Boys," one of them said, "anybody who could make a bridge out of them damn dog tents can beat us."

Prisoners were equally discouraged by the speed with which the railroad was repaired and put into operation behind retreating forces who had supposedly destroyed it. When news came that a tunnel had been wrecked by Rebel cavalry at the Federal rear, a prisoner said sadly, "It's no use, boys, Sherman's sure to carry a duplicate. The thing's all fixed by now."

Early in the campaign the artillery began to assume new importance. Cord's first experience with expert action was on a day when a battery of the Sixtieth Illinois came galloping to the assistance of his regiment as it was being driven from a hilltop by shells from an opposite fortification. Most of the Tenth had followed their commander to shelter in a ravine below, but Cord found refuge on higher ground where he could see the action. Four guns were brought up by foaming horses at the gallop. They were speedily set in place, unlimbered, and were ready to fire while the dust still fumed about them. A lieutenant sat by on his horse, snapping out orders.

"Number One, fire! Number Two, fire!" And presently came the command, "Fire at will!"

From where Cord watched as he hid behind a stump while enemy shells dropped nearby, he could see the first shot fall a little beyond the fortification. The second fell a little short of it. After that, every shell—signaled by a small puff of white smoke—dropped into the fort embrasure. In less than ten minutes the enemy battery had been silenced, and the Tenth was sent across the river to take possession of the demolished fort. Inside were guns that had been squarely hit.

"They could hunt squirrel with them cannon," Bill Foster said admiringly.

The Illinois battery was excelled only by the First Ohio, commanded by a handsome Prussian, Captain Dilger. He was known as "Leatherbreeches" because he always wore spotless doeskin trousers and shining top boots. He would often sight the cannon himself, and sometimes work it, always with deadly precision.

"Shust teeckle them fellows," was his usual expression, as he stepped back from the sights and clapped his hands smartly by way of orders.

Cord and Bill stood close beside him one day during the approach to Kennesaw Mountain. Leatherbreeches turned from sighting the guns to watch shell after shell drop cleanly into an enemy embrasure. He smiled his pleasure at the precision of his gunners, and also at the admiration of the boy and his companion.

"A gun, she shust like a gut dog," he said, as he looked at Cord. "Be kind to her, feed her, luf her, and she do shust vat you say, efry time."

"Whyn't you say somethin', Footey?" Bill asked, as they made their way back to camp.

"What's to say?" Cord was thinking of Chris, hoping that the woman he had given Chris to was being kind to him. Now, as each day saw a deeper advance into enemy country, with skirmishing of infantry and constant dueling of artillery, Cord felt less and less hope of ever seeing Chris again.

Under the June heat, maggots began to appear in everything, from men's wounds to the bacon and sugar in their mess boxes. Few of the men had been able to bathe or change their clothing since leaving Chattanooga and their bodies harbored not only the ordinary fleas they called "graybacks," but big red chiggers which would crawl through any cloth and bite viciously, often poisonously. Salt-water baths were almost the only remedy, but salt was too precious to use for bathing.

Cord, coming off ambulance duty one day, approached the sprawling group of tents where Mother Bickerdycke had her traveling laundry. He decided to ask her help in ridding his body of the chiggers and fleas that had been eating it. He had heard of Mother Bickerdycke, the brave and capable widow from Illinois who was largely responsible for the better-supplied hospital service in the field, but he had not made her acquaintance. She had followed the army from Chattanooga with a traveling laundry where she not only cleansed hospital equipment but wounded men as well. It was near the end of a hot dusty day and Cord's body was burning with insect bites. Seeing her standing by her tent, he went up to her and begged her for the use of the tub of water an attendant was about to empty out. Dirty as it was, the water looked more desirable then to Cord than anything he had seen in a long time.

"Why, bless you, son," she answered laughing, "that water has washed a major general, and fifteen privates! About enough for one tub, don't you think?"

"No, ma'am," Cord answered, impelled by his itching desperation, "please make it sixteen."

The earnestness of his plea softened Mother Bickerdycke into granting him the luxury of a fresh tub with herself to scrub his back. Before he dressed again, she gave him a handful of bacon rinds.

"Chiggers can't go bacon," she told him. "If you rub it

on and anoint your poor body with it every day, you'll nary have a chigger. Try it, my boy, and God bless you."

Cord disliked the process of anointing with hog, as the men called it, but it proved an effective remedy. It was promptly adopted by all the boys in the Drum Corps.

"I've heard tell that Uncle Billy gives himself the bacon bath," George Jay said.

That made it all right for them.

General Sherman lived as ruggedly as his men, and they respected and loved him for sharing the hardships of a soldier's life. When orders went forth that the men should camp without tents, he too was tentless, camping under the trees, sleeping on the ground, using only the crudest implements for his mess. General Thomas was totally different. Plump, dignified and comfort-loving, he insisted on shelter and seemliness at all times. Carefully dressed himself, he gave scrupulous attention to detail. Even during the men's tentless days, his headquarters' display of canvas was so prodigious that it was jokingly called "Thomas's Circus," or "Thomasville," or "Tom Town." When close to the enemy, its white conspicuousness had to be concealed by an elaborate camouflage of foliage and branches which the men became skilled in making. General Thomas had a chef to prepare the best food available, using proper dishes and a silver table service. Different as the two commanding generals were, the loyalty and affection of the men toward Pap Thomas was second only to that for Uncle Billy. Fighting Joe, as General Hooker was called, was perhaps the most impressive figure of all. Keen and alert in expression and bearing, he sat a fine horse and was always handsomely turned out in full major general's uniform and had an ornamental staff in attendance. To Cord, General Hooker appeared as the ideal and epitome of the perfect officer in command.

Much of the past month's march had been through the wooded and mountainous country back of the Oostenaula River. Now, as the armies converged on Kennesaw Mountain, they moved through open and fertile country. At times, their only possible shelter was secured by entrenching, at which they became expert with a variety of tools. When spades were not available, bayonets served, as did tin cups, canteen halves, forks, spoons, and often their own bare hands. In the midst of the heat of June there came days of torrential rains when they could only wallow miserably in the muck of their gopher holes, drying their clothes at feebly burning fires.

In such weather, General Sherman used a vacant house for headquarters. At night, by candlelight, the men could see him through the windows, pacing, pacing, pacing, head back, bristly bearded chin thrust stubbornly forward, hands plunged in his pockets.

"When Uncle Billy can't march by day, he marches all night," they told each other.

Kennesaw Mountain was the highest of three isolated hills; Pine Mountain and Lost Mountain being the others. They stood up abruptly in the open, somewhat rolling country approaching Atlanta. The hills had been thoroughly fortified and entrenched by the Confederate forces in slow retreat, and their batteries now swept the country on every side. Union approach had either to be very cautious or incontinently bold. General Sherman decided upon the latter, and the great army moved steadily forward. It had been one hundred thousand strong when the campaign began, but eighty miles of advance had cost them nine thousand men.

Spread over a front sometimes thirty miles in extent, the Union soldiers had not always realized their own impressive strength. But they realized fully the strength of the mountain that stood in their way and knew that it would not be taken without a bitter clash. They moved steadily forward in momentary expectation of enemy shelling, with the Tenth Michigan and the Sixtieth Illinois as front-line skirmishers. Enemy guns were ominously silent. They were able to gain the base of the mountain and dig themselves in, with only scattered musketry fire of sharpshooters to oppose them. Other units deployed and entrenched close by, and the wagon trains came up at night with rations. Barricading their trenches with logs and tree branches, they camped at the foot of Kennesaw for several days. Brief skirmishing expeditions sallied forth up the side of the mountain without opposition, and the men tried to still the odd suspense which the enemy's total quiet inspired in them.

At night they sang by their campfires, realizing that the morrow might mean the advance. Their songs often were more expressive of their loneliness than of their urge to battle.

> We're tenting tonight on the old camp ground,
> Give us a song to cheer
> Our weary hearts, a song of home,
> And friends we love so dear.
>
> Many are the hearts that are weary tonight,
> Wishing for the war to cease;
> Many are the hearts looking for the right,
> To see the dawn of peace.
> Tenting tonight, tenting tonight,
> Tenting on the old camp ground.

Men on the heights above were singing around their campfires, too, and the sound came drifting down on the warm June air with a wistfulness that made Cord think of the Negroes singing around the great orange fire at Stevenson, singing as if their hearts would break with the beauty of their song.

The men in blue started to sing a new song that had reached them from home. Everyone was singing it in the North and it had become a campground favorite:

> We shall meet, but we shall miss him,
> There will be one vacant chair;
> We shall linger to caress him,
> While we breathe our evening prayer.

But the men encamped on Kennesaw's height were not feeling that sentimental and down through the night came the lively strains of their own particular "Bonnie Blue Flag":

> We are a band of brothers, and native to the soil,
> Fighting for the property we gained by honest toil;
> And when our rights were threatened,
> The cry rose near and far,
> Hurrah for the Bonnie Blue Flag,
> That bears a single Star.
>
> Hurrah! Hurrah! for Southern Rights, Hurrah!
> Hurrah! for the Bonnie Blue Flag,
> That bears a single Star!

When taps finally sounded and the men of the different armies rolled up in their blankets to sleep, they felt some deep and comforting satisfaction. Sentiment had eased them, now sleep would refresh them. In the morning they would be able to respond to the drums, ready to fight up the slopes of Kennesaw or defend those slopes depending on whether blue or gray was the color of their uniforms.

But the morning dawned without gunfire, only the sun blazed over the countryside.

Cord and George were sitting in a trench playing poker with gun caps for chips when the first of the great artillery duels burst above them as though the mountain had suddenly turned volcanic. Instinctively they flattened themselves, though the shells screamed high over their heads and fell nowhere near them. For a long time their only desire was to stay flat, as the Union artillery gave answer and a shattering chorus of one hundred and fifty guns ensued. But by the time three or four giant sorties had taken place, always high overhead, the boys climbed up on the trench side and perched there like gophers to see what they could of the battle.

Union shells tore the ground and splintered rocks on the heights above them, while Confederate mortars threw up clouds of smoke that billowed fantastically around a whole area and filled the air with a choking sulphurous haze. Shells rushing overhead in swift succession exploded with a flash of fire, a sudden puff of cloud, then a whirring rain of fragments of iron could be heard thudding on the ground. When the artillery duel finally ceased, the boys crawled down into the trench to wait for orders.

Their drums were ready to sound the advance when orders came that relieved the Tenth from front-line duty that night. They were told to march back five miles and there to rest. The next day's orders were for the advance and long before daylight the drummers were out in full vigor. The men had been told to strip for action, so knapsacks and equipment were left with the wagons and they turned back to Kennesaw Mountain. The artillery was roaring as they began the advance, but presently it became silent. Orders rang out in the hot morning stillness for an infantry charge straight up the face of the mountain.

As men of the Tennessee and Cumberland armies pushed upward together, the mountain suddenly bristled and burned over all its upper half with the concentrated fire of twenty-five thousand muskets well entrenched. There was noise and confusion, men falling torn and shrieking, others stumbling over the dead or mangled bodies of their comrades, officers shouting, urging, pleading. Casualties steadily mounted until they numbered thousands. Ambulances dashed up into the chaos in a pitiful effort at salvage. Cord put his drum aside and turned to help bring in the wounded.

Under General Sherman's advance, provision for the wounded was better than it had ever been before. The new ambulances were two-horse spring wagons with room for eight or ten wounded to sit on benches around the sides, and for three to lie on the floor and three in the hammock stretchers that swung above. But nothing could make the plight of the wounded less than horrible on that blistering-hot day in that insect-ridden country. On one long jolting trip back to the field hospital, Cord was kept constantly busy fanning flies away lest wounds become black with them.

The attack was over in hardly more than an hour, and it was a total repulse. Nearly three thousand dead and wounded from the Union armies strewed the heat-wrapped and shell-torn mountainside. Hundreds of men had fallen at the brink of the enemy trenches. There they had met a jutting barricade, patterned after the deadly French *chevaux-de-frise*. Strong young trees, buried trench-deep and standing breast-high, had had their ends sharply pointed. Weighted with logs and brush, the barrier was unsurmountable even by the boldest of assaults. Men who reached it were hung up for slaughter on it. Behind the barrier, and still holding the height of the mountain, the enemy numbered their dead and wounded at some five hundred.

The Tenth spent the rest of the hot, dreadful day working around the mountain through the road jam which was always the aftermath of a battle. By nightfall they dug themselves into rifle pits southward near Marietta. For the next two days sharpshooting was incessant.

Cord longed for a gun. Sitting alone in a little clump of trees from which he could look out and up the hill to the enemy rifle pits, he occasionally saw a Johnny saunter across an opening directly above. It was the same man every time, for he wore a kind of shade hat unlike the rest. When Sergeant Low went down the line, leaving his gun lying not twenty feet from Cord, the temptation was irresistible. Cord crept down and got possession of the gun, then he found a place a little farther forward and nearer the skirmish line. There he rested the gun on a stump, sighted it, and waited, praying that the sergeant would not come back before he had had a chance to use the gun.

When the light hat appeared again, Cord fired.

No one noticed him, nothing happened, and so he continued to watch and wait.

After a little, the hat showed again. Again Cord fired, and this time the hat dropped suddenly out of sight. In another minute, three hatless Johnnies showed their heads above the spot where he had fallen. Yelling their wild, savage Rebel yell, they shouted defiance and the bullets began to shower about Cord. He bounded back to the shelter of his clump of trees and fired again, thrilled near to bursting with the sense of real soldiering at last. In his excitement he forgot to rest his gun. It kicked and threw him backwards into the scum and tangle of a stagnant pool.

When Sergeant Low returned, he rescued Cord from the muck and reclaimed his dripping gun. He said nothing, figuring that Cord had received enough punishment.

"Gosh, Cord, how'd it feel to get your man?" George Jay asked.

Cord had nothing to say. The ducking in the muddy pool had taken from him any gloating he might have had. He shrugged his shoulders. Suddenly he felt utter disgust for war in general, and for himself in particular.

By noon of the next day the stench of dead bodies on the mountain had grown unbearable. A truce of four hours was declared for burying them, with the victors claiming all guns and equipment. For a time, Yanks and Johnnies moved about together in the blazing sun, exchanging grim banter as they sorted the spoils, digging and filling and brushing over the shallow graves, mostly unmarked in their hurry. Four hours was not long enough and two more were granted; at the end of which they went back to their opposite rifle pits.

Two days of deadlock followed. On the morning of the third day, Confederate forces withdrew from Kennesaw Mountain back toward the Chattahoochie River. General Sherman's men followed, flanking, pursuing, digging in, until the enemy finally withdrew across the river. They wrecked the bridges, but fortified the bridgeheads on their side as if to make another stand. But there was no guarding that long, winding stretch of river against flanking pursuers. Before many hours, Sherman's scouts had found suitable crossing places above and below, and at them the pontoniers immediately set to work.

While awaiting bridges that hot July afternoon, thousands of Yankee soldiers seized the chance for their first good bath since leaving Chattanooga in early May. They swam and splashed in the Chattahoochie and sunned themselves on its banks. They boiled their clothes in coffeepots and kettles over hundreds of little fires at the water's edge. Toward sundown, Cord and George Jay and Ira Miles walked naked along the river while their clothes dried out after a thorough cooking. Turning a shady bend, they came upon their redbearded general, also naked, standing waist-deep in the river. An orderly swam near. A grinning teamster, who had brought his mules to water, sat on one of the braying beasts. All three chatted amiably, when the mules were quiet enough, as the general scrubbed himself.

"Great chance for the boys to get cleaned up for Atlanta," Uncle Billy was saying.

Cord and George gaped at the sight before them, envious of the two men who were sharing that hour with their commanding general. Reluctantly they turned away, too shy to invade further their general's attempted privacy.

"Gosh," George presently said what they all were thinking, "I'd follow Uncle Billy to hell."

"We may have to before we're done," Ira commented.

When their clothes had dried, they dressed and walked back to camp. An hour later they drummed for mess. Cord, looking off in the distance, could see the spires of Atlanta quivering miragelike through the haze of heat that lay over the countryside. Nearby, the sunset glow was reflected in the river. At that moment everything seemed at peace. It was hard to think that they might have to go through hell before they would be camping under the shadow of those sunset-gilded spires.

The respite of those few days' quiet camping in the groves along the river was welcome before the last grilling weeks of closing in upon Atlanta. Uncle Billy knew his men would march and fight the better for it.

On the morning of July 21st, drums sounded and the men fell in for the march on Atlanta. The end in sight was glorious, but the way to it—once they had crossed Peach Tree Creek —would be the way of the past months—skirmishing, marching, picketing, sniping, digging in. Next day came the report that Atlanta had fallen to the Federals. The men of the Michigan Tenth and the Sixtieth Illinois marched forward at a reckless pace, with colors waving, bugles calling and drums setting the quickstep. Three and a half miles from Atlanta they found that the report was false. That night they bivouacked in the open and moved into the front line at an early hour the next day; breastworks were thrown up, an abatis was made, and there they stayed while heavy firing took place on both sides.

The men of the Tenth knew that they were a small part in a complex wheeling movement of three great armies that were besieging Atlanta. As a unit of the Army of the Cumberland, their task was to engage the enemy's attention without directly attacking, while keeping themselves always ready to resist a possible counterstroke. The Army of the Tennessee moved rapidly around and outside them, its task to accomplish the isolation of Atlanta by destroying the railroad to the east. The Army of the Ohio moved inside them, striking at railroad lines to the south and west, and keeping itself ready to link up with the two other armies as crisis might demand.

From their bivouac, the Tenth moved out one day in light order to assist in repulsing a Rebel attack; the next day they moved in heavy order, carrying all their equipment. They made a circuit of eight miles, passing their own breastworks late in the day. Orders were to march until midnight, and so they kept on. Weariness and heat were their opponents, but the men marched. Roll after roll of the drums, sounding steadily through the long dark hours, carried them along.

Ira Miles detailed the drummers for duty during the night. Cord had learned to sleep on his feet, even when marching, and to come awake when the order came for him to carry the roll so another drummer could rest. Sometimes Cord's fingers were so stiff and mechanical that they would not bend for him to put the sticks away.

"You've got to make yourself rest," Ira said to him gently when he saw Cord's twitching fingers beating a silent roll against his frayed coat. "You've got to get those fingers quiet, Cordie, so you can get them to drum again when I call on you an hour from now."

Cord looked up at Ira and nodded, then he brought his rebellious fingers into salute.

By midnight, when they stopped to pitch camp, some of

the men were so exhausted that they dropped down to sleep where they were standing.

The next day they lay in line until noon. Carrying out a skirmish, they encountered a Rebel detachment and pressed them back a mile. The following day, relieved by the Sixtieth Illinois, the Tenth was able to retire to the breastworks that had been constructed several days before. Day after day during a hot July and into a hotter August, the marches and the skirmishes went on. Men were worn out by constant moving, constant digging in behind new fortifications, picket duty and field reconnaissance. Their casualties had been light. They wondered what they would be when the attack for which all this was preparation got under way.

A casualty was a body to be buried, a number on an official record; unless it happened to be a friend. Then a casualty was a hole in the heart, made by the same bullet. Taking away everything, it left only an emptiness—a hurting, aching emptiness, a horror that never really let go, a terrible questioning. Why did this have to happen to him?

Cord was sitting in the drummers' tent one afternoon trying to write a letter home, trying to think of something to say that would be news, when George Jay was carried in and laid on his cot.

Ira Miles stood beside him. "He was in that apple orchard when a sniper's bullet got him."

The surgeon came and took one look at George. "Shot through the heart," he said to Ira. "You'll have to take care of him quick. Orders have just come from headquarters to move before sundown."

Ira looked around desperately. "Get some of the men, Cordie. Tell them to bring shovels with them."

Cord could believe neither his eyes nor his ears, but he found himself automatically carrying out Ira's orders.

They buried George while he was still warm. Ira put

Cord's drum over his shoulder and pushed the sticks between his fingers, but Cord could not make his hands beat the last roll for his friend. Desolation swept over him, dark as a starless night, and deep as a well without a bottom.

In the distance a bugle was blowing. The drums of the other companies had commenced to roll. Men were starting to assemble. The drummer boy of Company F held his sticks over the batter head of his drum. The men of the Michigan Tenth moved on to their new position.

That night, when the adjutant prepared his official report, he listed only one casualty—George Jay, musician.

On the 25th of August the bold move began which was to bring the capture of Atlanta. At General Sherman's orders, the Fourteenth Corps withdrew from its position west of the city. Cutting loose from the base of supplies on the Chattahoochie with only ten days' rations, they marched to the south and east toward Jonesboro. Unable to believe that an army would deliberately separate itself from its base, the enemy mistook this maneuver for retreat; not realizing their error until it was too late to remedy it. At the last, a desperate attempt was made to intercept the Union advance by dispatching two corps under Generals Hardee and Cleburne to Jonesboro. On September first, the Fourteenth Corps came into sharp encounter with the Confederates.

They were crossing an open field toward a ravine when enemy guns opened fire from emplacements at the summit of the high farther bank. The First Division, moving at the rear, withdrew into a wood for shelter and to form lines of battle. The advance brigade charged ahead against Cleburne's corps which was drawn up for action in the field beyond. Cleburne's division prided itself that it had never been driven, and after only an instant's uncertainty before the fierce momentum of the attack, turned upon the onrushing columns with such savage fury that they were routed in confusion.

At that moment the Second Brigade moved out from its wooded shelter with its battle lines completely formed. It, too, was equally prideful of the fact that it had never been driven. After a half hour of desperate, close fighting, Cleburne's division crumpled back helplessly before the determined onslaught.

The Tenth, with Major Burnett commanding, was in the thick of the charge, clambering boldly up the side of the ravine toward the enemy works, when the major was shot and killed. The lines wavered a little amid the deadly rain of grape and canister, before the officer nearest Major Burnett sprang to the fore.

"Come on, me brave lads," shouted Captain Dunphy, an Irishman who had been twice promoted for bravery. "Come on, me brave lads. Michigan forever! Glory or a wooden leg!"

The men cheered and charged on furiously behind their captain.

Cord, standing with the other drummers where the surgeons were setting up a hospital tent, saw the charge and heard Captain Dunphy's bold words.

"Michigan forever! Glory or a wooden leg!" Cord shouted.

The boys picked up their drumsticks and beat out the charge, raising such a daddy-mammy as they felt their men must hear above the whistling bullets and the unearthly yells made by the Rebel soldiers.

Captain Dunphy scrambled ahead, first over the parapet with six men close behind him, to capture a full stand of colors. The rest swarmed up and over to support them. Enemy lines fell back before the bayonets of the Michigan Tenth.

In an hour, two lines of works had been captured, and an

entire regiment taken prisoner. Seventy-one men of the Tenth lay dead upon the field and there were, as yet, uncounted wounded.

The Drum Corps worked through most of the night, helping to bring in the wounded and care for them. As they worked, they heard strange distant thunder from the direction of Atlanta, twenty miles away, and they wondered if things had gone wrong. They dropped down to sleep without knowing, too exhausted then to care. At daylight the grim business of burying the dead began. And still they did not know what the thunder signified. It was not until the next day that the good news reached them.

General Sherman had sent out an exultant telegram the previous night: SO ATLANTA IS OURS, AND FAIRLY WON. Cord's father and mother knew of the victory before Cord did.

"But we went through hell to get it," Ira Miles said as he tightened the ropes on his drum and got it ready for parade.

It was a red-letter day for the Tenth when, before the massed divisions of the Fourteenth Corps, General Thomas cited them for conspicuous gallantry. The general sat his horse before them, stocky of figure, sandy of whiskers, and beaming of countenance when Captain Dunphy presented him with the captured colors. The captain was cited, too, and promoted to command of the regiment. Then congratulatory orders were read for all from General Sherman, General Grant, and President Lincoln.

None knew what lay before them as they swung off toward Atlanta on the march the next day, with full fanfare of drums at the fore; but they were ready for anything.

"Come on, me brave lads!" Ira Miles had called, as he lined them up to lead. "Come on, me brave lads! Michigan forever! Glory or a wooden leg!"

They cheered and fell into their stride. Captain Dunphy's words had become the regimental slogan.

CHAPTER XI

THEY MARCHED SEVEN MILES to White Hall, where they went into camp for a month. The late summer days were hot and humid, fighting was over for a time, discipline was relaxed. Men could leave camp without a pass. The freedom was almost like being on furlough.

Cord and Jennie went off to see Atlanta. They found it a gaunt, depressing sight as they prowled among shattered and forsaken buildings interspersed with those that had been unharmed. One hotel was doing business with an unexploded shell embedded in its wooden front.

"Risky business, I'd say," Jennie remarked.

Cord had no words for the horror he felt.

"But Uncle Billy hasn't finished with Atlanta," Jennie said. "There won't be anything left when we push on to the sea!" His words were boastful.

Cord wondered if he wanted to see it then.

As they wandered through the city they saw places where

the citizens who had lived in exposed areas had built dugouts for themselves, like the cyclone cellars some of the soldiers from the West knew well. They saw a railroad cut near the city's edge which had been burrowed and delved into on both sides, with steps dug to connect the caves and gopher holes in which people had taken refuge. It looked like a cliff dwellers' colony.

"Gosh," said Jennie, "we thought we had it tough enough, but the Johnnies have had it lots worse!"

"They always do," Cord answered, thinking of the corncobs in the haversack he had found at Chickamauga Station.

Learning that some of their wounded from the battle at Jonesboro had been brought to Atlanta for care, the boys set out to find them. They trudged the rounds of the temporary hospitals located in abandoned store buildings into which rows upon rows of cots had been set. In one, as Cord and Jennie cautiously looked down a long ward, two men of the Tenth recognized and called to them.

"Hi, boys," said George Rose, who had lost a leg, "Michigan forever! Glory and a wooden leg!"

"It's glory and a glass eye for me, I guess," said the other as he touched his bandaged forehead.

The men were gloating with victory, no matter what the cost had been to themselves.

"Michigan forever," echoed the boys.

There were many sutlers on the outskirts of Atlanta, among them some ovenmen with whom Cord and Jennie entered into an arrangement for a pie business. Buying pies at twenty-five cents each, they sold them at camp for fifty, doubling their money by a walk of seven miles each way. They sold newspapers, too, whenever they could get them. There was enormous interest at camp in the fiery correspondence between Generals Hood and Sherman regarding the latter's demand for civilian evacuation of Atlanta. Cord came to know by heart many pungent sentences from Uncle Billy's letters defending his position.

"Atlanta is a fortified town, was stubbornly defended, and fairly captured," General Sherman wrote. "As captors we have a right to it. . . . You cannot qualify war in harsher terms than I will. War is cruelty and you cannot refine it. . . . But you cannot have peace and division of our country. If the United States submits to a division it will not stop but will go on until we reap the fate of Mexico, which is eternal war."

Mute evidence to General Sherman's words was in the tragic caravan of exile that streamed past the camp at White Hall day after day as a steady procession of Federal wagons transported those citizens who chose to go to the refugee camp at Rough and Ready a few miles farther south. The wagons were piled with feather beds, fine old furniture, family portraits, as well as humbler belongings—the heaped-up remnants of what stricken old men and women, frightened mothers, and crying children had once called home.

"What are they going away for?" Cord asked.

"Didn't I tell you Uncle Billy hadn't finished with Atlanta?" Jennie replied.

They were walking back to camp with a basket of pies when a wagon passed them with its pitiful human load. A pair of noisy poll parrots got out of hand, to the terrible fright of the young lady who held the cage.

"Polly! Polly!" shrieked one, as the wagon went by. "Look at the damn Yankees! Look at the damn Yankees!"

"Damn Yankees! Damn Yankees!" screeched the other, still more wildly, while their young mistress looked as though she expected instant death from the hands of the wagon driver or the two boys in faded blue who were trudging along the road carrying a basket between them.

Cord and Jennie laughed loudly at the parrot's name calling.

News reached the camp at White Hall that General Hood had swung his army back and was marching and destroying in Tennessee. Then, on the 28th of September, orders came to march to Atlanta and take cars to Chattanooga. The Tenth marched, though not without some grumbling, as it seemed like going backward to return to earlier campgrounds rather than marching on to the sea. They lay aboard the unmoving train all night, many of them sleeping on top of the cars because inside they were foully dirty. At seven in the morning they began to move. All day long the train ran slowly through the Georgia countryside over which they had advanced so laboriously a few months ago. That night they slept again on the top of the cars, but as the train was moving at its leisurely pace they linked themselves together so they would not roll off. They reached Chattanooga at noon but were ordered to remain on board. Presently they moved on to Stevenson, where they detrained and bivouacked on the campground of the year before.

"Hi, Footey," Bill Foster called as he came up with Cord near the old guardhouse, "wanta bunk down with me in the lockup tonight?"

"Sure, if you'll get the gingerbread and Brazil nuts."

The next day the cars took them to Florence, Alabama, where they had a glimpse of General Rosecrans, who had just come up with a corps from the southwest. After camping there briefly, they were ordered to board the cars again. They spent a week being shunted about through various Alabama towns where cavalry operations were in progress which might need their support. Being held in reserve began to seem fully as wearisome as marching, and not nearly so interesting.

One day, in the village of Huntsville, Cord and Jennie spent a whole lazy afternoon lying under the trees that were just beginning to turn beside a beautiful little pool. It was fed by a spring that gushed from a rocky ledge and its crystalline depths appeared to go to the center of the earth. It seemed like peace, after the hurly-burly of the cars. Neither one spoke. Long quiet minutes went by with no sound save the whispering drop of a leaf to float silently on the still, blue surface of the pool.

Finally Cord said, "There's not many places I want to see again, but I sure would like to come back to this little pool, an' just set the way we're doin' now."

"Maybe we'll come back together, Cordie."

"Maybe," Cord said slowly, thinking of Jimmie Tyson, and Vandie, and George Jay. He thought of Chris, too, and then his thoughts were of Old Lacey. At least he was one person the war wouldn't take away. Pop was safe in Michigan, waiting for the boys to get back and tell him how they won the war, following their marches on the same map he once had hung up in the drummers' tent.

Toward evening, a group of Negroes came to the spring. They carried water jugs to be filled, and they balanced them on their heads as they walked with lithe, free steps. The boys watched, marveling at the ease with which they placed the filled and heavy jugs upon their heads and walked away as carelessly as when the jugs had been empty.

On their way back to the cars they passed a roadside shanty from which two old women came out to gaze at them. They were witchlike creatures with stringy hair and leathery wrinkled skin. Both of them were dipping snuff as they stared at the boys.

Cord, feeling sociable, asked, "Any Johnnies around here?"

They glared at him with fury in their eyes.

"You damn Yankees'll soon find out if they's any Johnnies,"

cackled one of them, while the other laughed shrilly, for all the world like the poll parrots.

"Guess that's our name all right around here," Jennie said.

That night, at camp, the boys tried to show some of the men how the Negroes had balanced the water jugs on their heads. They filled two buckets and started to march through the camp, but they nearly drowned for their exhibition and the men laughed at them until Jennie wished he had some of the poll parrots' language to hurl at them.

A few days later the brigade returned to Chattanooga and from there was dispatched to Atlanta to continue the destruction of the city; but the Michigan Tenth was retained as escort for Major General Schofield on his way back from a military mission in Ohio to his troops somewhere in Georgia. Orders came to the drummers' tent that Coridon Foote and John Jennings were to be detailed as orderlies to General Schofield and that a horse was awaiting each one, as well as a saber.

Cord hung up his drum and donned the belt from which his saber hung. No matter how tight he wore it, or how high, the saber still dragged on the ground; but he did not care. Now, when he saluted, he felt the full tide of military importance flood through him. Dropping his hand, he placed it on the saber's hilt. For two years he had felt himself to be every inch a veteran; now he felt every foot a soldier.

The boys rode with the general and his staff for the next forty-eight hours. One of them held his horse while he mounted or dismounted, while the other held his stirrup. When General Schofield stopped the first night at a house along the way, the boys slept on the ground outside and took turns at sentry duty. The general was a pleasant, mild-faced man with a long dark beard. There was a quiet dignity about him. His words were few, but they carried conviction.

At noon of the third day, General Schofield came from a

house where he had stopped to eat and stood talking with a member of his staff while Cord held his stirrup, waiting for the general to mount.

"The troops we are looking for," said the general, "should now be moving on a parallel road about five miles from here, carrying the flag of the Twenty-third. Take my orderly, Major, and ride across to find them. But see that you keep a sharp lookout for guerrillas."

"Yes, sir." The major mounted his horse and beckoned to Cord to follow him.

Cord's horse was tethered nearby. He went over to it as quickly as he could, hitching his belt up as he walked so the saber would not drag too much. Soon he was galloping down the road after the major. Cord hoped that the major was watching for guerrillas, as he had all he could do to keep his smaller horse up with the major's larger one. After riding hard for an hour, they stopped to reconnoiter at a place where cavalry horses had lately been feeding.

"We'll have to look sharp now, Foote. If these are guerrillas, it'll be too bad for us."

"Yes, sir," Cord said. He had a sinking feeling at the pit of his stomach. Much as he had always admired the cavalry, he had always wondered what a man did when his horse was shot under him. Cord felt himself turning rigid with the contemplation of such a moment, then he slid his hand onto his saber hilt. It was his weapon now. He would have felt safer with his slingshot, but that was in his haversack at camp.

"We'll cool our horses, Foote, but keep on the ready."

"Yes, sir."

They walked their horses for a while, side by side, not saying anything, but watching, watching, trying to see through every clump of trees, and around every bush and boulder. At a bend in the road they came within view of a log house. Ten or a dozen horses were tethered in front of it.

"There they are, sir," gasped Cord.

"Yes, there they are. Friend or foe, that's the question." The major ruminated for a moment. "Well, Foote," he said, "the best thing for us to do is to gallop our hardest, straight past them, and if they follow, try to keep ahead of them until we reach our troops down the line. Come on. Mount up. Let's go now—fast!"

What if there were no troops down the line? Cord wondered.

They spurred their horses and set off on the turf-grown roadside to make less sound. Cord's heart pounded until it nearly choked him. Faster they galloped, and faster until they were almost even with the house. The tethered horses plunged with fright and neighed shrilly as they passed. Cord found himself breathing more freely, for at least they now had a head start. Galloping on, he heard a door slam in the house behind him. He looked back, then spurred his horse harder as he saw four men walk out, all in uniforms of Federal blue.

"Hi, Major, they're ours!" he shouted, almost foolish with relief. "They're ours."

The major did not stop. Leaning low on his horse's neck he turned his head and called back, "Guerrillas often wear stolen Federal uniforms. Keep up the pace until we join our men."

Cord spurred his horse. Looking back again he could see that the men had mounted and were in pursuit of them.

Cord's horse was breathing heavily, the major's had begun to falter when, in the distance ahead, they spied a welcome cloud of dust.

"Troops moving," the major said. He coaxed his horse into a new burst of speed.

Cord pounded on, glancing back now and then, and finally

comforted by the fact that their pursuers had given up the chase. At a crossroads he caught up with the major, who had stopped to examine the distant troops with his glasses. Their horses, heaving and foam-flecked, tossed their heads as if impatient to join those on the road ahead, a road that ran at right angles to the one they had been traveling.

"Fine business, Foote!" the major exulted. "Isn't that the flag of the old Twenty-third?"

Cord looked more carefully, then he nodded; but he was puzzled as to why what they had just done should be called fine business.

"I've found out what General Schofield wanted to know. Let's get on."

When they reached the moving troops, the major reported to the officers commanding. The information apparently was important, for they received it thoughtfully, and the word "guerrillas" was mentioned more than once.

Cord, dismissed from immediate duty, edged around to join the cavalry. They were, to his surprise and delight, the Michigan Fourth, detailed to accompany the Twenty-third Infantry on its march. Among them he found many old friends from home. He rode with them the rest of the day, until they reached field headquarters where General Schofield and his staff had bivouacked.

Cord reported to his commander and the general's "Well done" surprised him no less than the major's; but it gratified him even more. He was sorry only that it was followed by orders which meant that his detail as a staff orderly was accomplished. The next day when they closed in with the Tenth, meeting approximately at noon at a designated four corners, Foote and Jennings were to rejoin their regiment. So the boys polished their sabers and rubbed their horses down for the last time, and when morning dawned they donned their drums and led off with the Tenth on the road that was heading back to Atlanta.

At Centreville, the Tenth rejoined the Second Brigade and the Fourteenth Corps. Mail was waiting for them, and pay, and ballots so they might cast their votes in the forthcoming presidential election.

Cord was denied the privilege of a ballot. Once considered too young to be a soldier, he was definitely thought too young to be a voter. There was no ruse he could adopt that would make him appear to be voting age. He would have given a good deal to be able to cast his vote for Mr. Lincoln. There was scarcely a man in Sherman's advancing armies who did not realize the importance of Lincoln's re-election to each one of them. With another President in the White House, the war might be settled by a compromise. Men who had been fighting for the Union for three weary years did not want to see that happen. Just as Lincoln had to be re-elected for the sake of the Union, so did Sherman have to win a conclusive victory for the sake of Mr. Lincoln.

General Grant had given his sanction to Uncle Billy when he said to him, "Go on as you proposed." The men had read the words in a newspaper account and they knew that their commanding general's glance would not waver, his heart would not falter, until he had cut through Georgia to the sea. Nor would theirs. Together they would give to Mr. Lincoln the victory upon which his presidency might depend.

Now, as they sat around their campfires at Centreville, after having cast their ballots, they sang some of the songs that had been written at the time of Lincoln's first call for volunteers, and second call in 1863. Many of the men had marched away from their home towns to those songs.

"Way down in old Varginni, I suppose you all do know,
They have tried to bust the Union but they find it is no go,

> The Yankee boys are starting out de Union for to sabe,
> And we're going down to Washington,
> To fight for Uncle Abe."

Cord might not be able to vote, but he knew he could drum and he put the passionate patriotism he was feeling into the sound he was making, increasing the tempo for the chorus and tucking in a roll that might have done for an infantry charge.

> "Rip, Rap, Flip, Flap, strap your knapsacks on your back
> For we're agwine to Washington
> To fight for Uncle Abe."

But a good many of the men sang the word "vote" in place of the word "fight."

When the Fourteenth Corps proceeded toward Atlanta, it was with orders to destroy the railroad as they advanced. The men fell to with grim and determined vigor. This was a part of the victory Uncle Billy needed to shorten the war and keep Mr. Lincoln in the White House. Cord had his own reason for wanting to see the war end soon and conclusively. In another three months his enlistment would run out and he would no longer be able to be a part of the war. He intended to do everything he could to hasten the end. Marching at the head of his company, he beat his drum in concert with the other drummers. The sound rapped out and reverberated through the cool autumn air. It seemed to get inside the men themselves. Feet stepped forward, wheels began to turn, horses dug their hoofs into the earth and mules pulled. The Tenth was on its way.

The move was a bold one, as General Sherman's moves invariably were. Again, they cut themselves off from their base of supplies, and this time in far more daring fashion than when they were marching to Jonesboro. The brigade spread itself along the railroad track for about a mile. Men, picked for the task, pried rails from the ties with strong young trees that had been cut down and swung over logs for leverage. As the rails were loosened, other men tore up the ties, cording them in hollow squares which they set on fire, using fence rails for kindling and plenty of oil. The steel rails were then laid across the fires and heated until they were red hot. When molten, they sagged in the middle and were useless for repair; but at General Sherman's explicit direction they were to be lifted red hot and twisted around trees or telegraph poles—"Sherman's gimlets" they were called.

Thus they moved, mile after mile, day after day, in a steady program of destruction which left a smoking, smoldering wake behind them. When they arrived at Atlanta, they saw a smoking, smoldering ruin before them. It was a skeleton city, its business and industrial section a forest of blackened chimneys.

Some of the men were silent as they sat around their campfires outside Atlanta. Others remembered what General Sherman had written to the people of the Confederacy:

> If the people protest against my barbarity and cruelty, I will answer that war is war, and you yourselves have elected to settle this issue by war. . . . Once admit the Union, I and this army become at once your protectors and supporters, shielding you from danger, let it come from whatever quarter it may. . . . Until then, you might as well appeal against the thunderstorm as against these terrible hardships of war.

Grim as the business of destruction was, there was not a man of those who marched with Uncle Billy who did not feel but that he was right.

CHAPTER XII

IT WAS RAW AND COLD on the morning of November 15, 1864, when General Sherman's orders were read and 62,000 men were informed of the march into the heart of enemy territory from Atlanta to the sea. Telegraph lines were to be cut. There would be no cracker line to sustain them. They were to march fifteen miles a day, living off the country and giving back "a devastation more or less ruthless." The news for which they all had been waiting had recently come over those telegraph lines—Mr. Lincoln had been re-elected. "Three cheers for Old Abe!" they had shouted until they were hoarse; now it was "Three cheers for Uncle Billy!"

"I'd follow him into the sea if he asked me to," Ira Miles said.

"Wherever Uncle Billy leads is the place for me," Jennie added.

Cord said nothing. George Jay had been willing to go through hell, and he had found it in an apple orchard.

The Michigan Tenth, as part of the left wing of a flanking movement, received its orders to proceed in an easterly direction toward Augusta. The right wing, which included cavalry and two infantry corps, would proceed south toward Macon. Within seven days, both wings would converge upon the newly established state capital at Milledgeville. That night, by the glow of Atlanta burning, men packed forty rounds of ammunition in their belts and three days' rations in their haversacks. In the morning they rolled up their blankets and were ready for action. Almost no other luggage was allowed except a coffeepot and a stewpan for each group of messmates.

The vast expedition began to move shortly after noon on the 16th of November with bands playing and men singing the "Battle Hymn of the Republic." Cresting a hill near Decatur, not long after, the drummers of the Tenth looked out upon the undulating blue ranks that reached for miles ahead of them. Fifteen thousand gun barrels were glinting in the sun; fifteen thousand voices were singing:

"Mine eyes have seen the glory of the coming of the Lord;
He is trampling out the vintage where the grapes
of wrath are stored . . ."

It was a portentous thunder of song, accented by rattling drums and marching feet. Looking back, the drummers could see stretching behind them five miles of white-topped wagons and a huge drove of cattle. Anything seemed possible to an army like that.

Ira Miles nodded his head proudly. "And just think, Cordie, every road out of Atlanta to the north and the east must look like this one."

The second day's march was made through continuous heavy rain. The Tenth, detailed to drive the great herd of unwilling cattle at the rear, did not get into camp until after nine that night. They were wet, cold and hungry, and plastered with mud from head to foot.

"But we're not near so cold and wet as we would have been without these new poncho blankets they issued to us in Atlanta," Ira said.

Cord, Ira Miles, and Jennie still wore their ponchos as they poked about trying to nurse a fire for bacon and coffee. Most of the wood was wet and the rain kept coming down. No matter how they blew and poked and fanned, it all seemed to be in vain. A soldier, wearing an overcoat with a cape and a slouch hat drawn well down over his eyes, had been watching them.

"Try a poncho over it, boys," he said, as he stepped nearer them, "and I think you'll get it."

Cord scrambled out of his poncho and dropped to his knees to blow, while Ira and the soldier held the poncho over the fire. Jennie added a handful of dry twigs which he had been harboring. Cord blew and blew. At last a spark was roused, then a few flames began to flicker. Cord grinned up into the red-bearded face of the stranger.

"There, you have it," said the soldier, quite as pleased as they were.

"Thank you, Uncle Billy," said Cord, a little breathless at his boldness as he took the poncho from the general's outstretched hand.

With the merest hint of a smile, General Sherman nodded and walked away.

Cord put his head through the slit of his poncho. "I knew who it was all the time."

"That's Uncle Billy for you," Ira Miles commented as he placed the frying pan over the fire, "always knows more than us fellows. Even when it comes to gettin' wet wood to burn, he can show us somethin'."

The next day brought the beginning of good weather

which continued almost unbroken throughout the campaign —clear, sunny, exhilarating. Drums and bugles sounded reveille at five o'clock, and soon after, the twenty or thirty foragers detailed from the brigade for the day set out to scour the surrounding plantations for food. They rode on horses or mules, with wagons following. Sometimes they returned in an hour or two with an abundant supply; more often they remained out all day. With other foraging parties they acted as a kind of self-constituted skirmishing line, bewildering the lurking enemy and effectively protecting the marching columns.

Foragers' orders were strict, authorizing the confiscation of "whatever is needed by the command," but forbidding them to enter the "dwellings of inhabitants or commit any trespass"; urging discrimination "between the rich who are usually hostile, and the poor or industrious, usually neutral or friendly." They were also urged to "refrain from abusive or threatening language . . . and endeavor to leave with each family a reasonable portion of their maintenance."

The main column of the brigade got in motion by six o'clock, regiments assuming in rotation rear-guard duty one day and advance guard the next. Advance guard was always the more adventurous detail and was craved by the men above any but forage duty. Rear guard was the more arduous, particularly when the advance went through swampy regions where roads had to be corduroyed before the wagons could get through. There were days when the Tenth did not get in from rear-guard duty until two or three in the morning; then as advance guard they had to be ready to lead off in a few hours.

Whenever possible, the regiment camped on a hillside. In the early dusk, campfires could be seen glowing all along the slope and in the sweep of the valley. From the fires rose the aromatic smell of wood smoke and the pungent odor of cooking. Later on, the fires drew men around them to sing and talk together, or lie and listen to the singing of others. The songs they sang those nights, as they gazed up at the stars or into the ruddy coals of a campfire, were different from the martial songs of the daytime. "Farewell, Farewell, My Own True Love" and "Aura Lee" echoed often through the night. Bands serenaded each other, or sometimes massed together to play General Sherman's favorites. Invariably they ended with the mellifluous strains of "The Blue Juniata." As the song melted into silence, bugles and drums began to sound taps. Up the hillside and through the valley the fires died down to quivering ash; in their tents or rolled up in blankets on the ground the soldiers slept.

Morning came quickly with its echoing and re-echoing reveille of drums and bugles. Thin, gray, vertical columns of wood smoke spiraled upward from hundreds of fires. The pleasant fragrance of coffee and bacon cooking diffused itself in the frosty air. There was clangor and gusto of movement everywhere as unit after unit formed in marching order to swing away roaring one of their favorite songs.

"This is great," Cord said to Ira. "This is what it should be like all the time."

"Well," Ira agreed, "this is a part of the war."

As they made their way deeper into enemy country, they came into regions that had been systematically slashed. Advance guard grew increasingly more arduous. Marching hours were lost as felled trees and piles of underbrush had to be cleared from the roads. But the weather was good, they had an objective, and as they moved steadily forward they feasted on the fat of the land. Turkey, pork, chicken, beef, yams, honey, became now their daily fare, as well as butter, eggs, pickles, preserves, as they helped themselves to the stores in smokehouses and plantation kitchens. Now there were times when the Georgia campaign seemed like a gorgeous holiday, a skylarking reward for past hardships.

Foragers interpreted their orders more and more broadly. It was not often possible to "confiscate" without "entering," and the nature of their commission involved violence of a sort. As Bill Foster said, "It ain't so easy to coax a pig out'n its pen to be pork." They might "refrain from abusive or threatening language," but Yankee acquisitiveness could not be contained.

Cord, never officially designated as a forager, smuggled himself along with Bill Foster one day on a foraging expedition. Finding no pork or poultry anywhere, and only one enormous yam, they took ramrods and decided to look for buried treasure in the lawn surrounding an old plantation house. To their amazement, they unearthed a chest of finery and family heirlooms. Bill dressed himself in an evening gown, and Cord, not to be outdone, put one on, too. Laughing at the spectacle they had made of themselves, they paraded up and down in their silks and laces; while from the colonnaded porch the young ladies of the family watched them helplessly. They had expected abuse and were prepared for it; what they witnessed was torture, bewildering and even more terrible than violence might have been.

As Cord and Bill trailed by in their low-cut gowns, one of the young ladies could stand it no longer. "You dastardly brutes," she cried out, "if my brother were here you wouldn't dare do this!"

Bill gazed at her flashing eyes with mingled admiration and scorn. "Aw, shucks," he said, "mebbe I been swimmin' with your brother in the Tennessee, an' he's good an' plenty sick o' this here war. If you gals will just lay off o' your singin' an' wavin' the bonnie blue flag, an' give the poor fellas a chance to come down to earth, I bet your brothers'll be home for the spring plowin'."

"Yes, an' mighty glad of it," said Cord.

"Sure," Bill added, "you Dixie belles and beaus started this war, but us 'damn Yankees' is goin' to end it, and that right soon!"

Bill and Cord swaggered about some more, then they got ready to leave. They stuffed pieces of the family silver into their haversacks, peeled off their borrowed finery and left it strewn on the porch steps, and returned to camp carrying between them the three-foot-long yam, which Bill gave to Cord. "You can sit on one end of it," he said, "while the other end's roastin' in the fire."

Some of the foragers returned to camp that night with live young pigs and fat hens, as well as tubs of molasses and barrels of flour. Others returned dressed up in satins, velvets, and old regimentals confiscated from family chests. Men guffawed at each other, play-acted, and mocked the pretense put on by their fellows. The camp looked as if a fancy dress ball were being held, and a riotous one at that.

Ira Miles shook his head dismally. "It's an awful thing when men git too big for their own britches an' have to dress up in clothes that don't belong to 'em."

"They're just a lot o' young roughnecks halloweening," Cord said. "Decent roughnecks, really."

"Decent?" Ira laughed bitterly. "They's another word I'd use—"

Whatever it was, it was lost in the noisy horseplay and shouts of laughter that resounded as the men paraded before each other in their stolen finery.

"I wouldn't like to see you actin' like that, Cordie." Ira shook his head again.

Cord said nothing. He was beginning to feel ashamed of himself for what he had done that afternoon with Bill Foster, and he hoped with all his heart that Ira would never find out. He put his head in his hands, wondering why it was that he did things he didn't really want to do when he was with Bill. He felt himself aching with loneliness—for Old Lacey, for shaggy Chris, for George Jay, even for Tommy Branch. At the thought of Tommy he brightened. Tommy, from all reports, was still with his father, still riding his little gray donkey. When the two flanking wings converged, he might meet up with Tommy again and they could go adventuring.

Ira put his hand on Cord's shoulder. "It's Michigan forever, Cordie, and time to sound taps."

Cord responded to his cue. "Glory or a wooden leg," he said as he went to get his drum. He hoisted the belt over his shoulder and took his sticks from between the ropes. There were some days that he did not like to bring to an end, but this was not one of them. The sooner today ended the better, and taps would do it. Later, as he lay on his cot with wide-open eyes staring into the darkness, Cord wondered why it was that war made a fellow do things against his own nature. Yet war called out the best and bravest, too. Trying to find an answer, he fell asleep.

All along the way, Negroes swarmed out to greet the blue-coated soldiers, hailing them as if they were delivering angels. Men from the West had felt they were fighting for the preservation of the Union; men from the abolitionist East had felt they were fighting for the emancipation of the slave. Now, as many of them met the Negro for the first time, they gained new feeling for the tragedy of his situation. His humor was something they could appreciate and use, and the men took over many Negro songs as popular marching tunes.

With colors flying and drums sounding, the Michigan Tenth marched out one morning singing jauntily:

"Nicodemus, the slave, was of African birth,
And was bought for a bag full of gold.
He was reckoned as part of the salt of the earth,
And he died years ago, very old.
'Twas his last sad request as we laid him away
In the trunk of an old hollow tree,
'Wake me up,' was his charge, 'at the first break of day,
Wake me up for the great jubilee!' "

When the refrain came, they shouted it lustily and the drums rattled out louder than before:

"There's a good time coming, it's almost here,
'Twas long, long, long on the way.
Then run and tell 'Lijah to hurry up Pomp,
And meet us by the gum tree down in the swamp,
For to wake Nicodemus today."

From abandoned plantations or miserable hiding places, the Negroes streamed to march along with the advancing soldiers. Women shuffled over the ground with children in their arms and more children tagging close to their skirts. Men led donkeys with children astride them, and babies' faces often peeped out from ragged saddlebags or panniers. White-haired household slaves limped with weariness along the dusty road.

"De day o' jubilo is sure come," they said, their faces alight no matter how tired they might be, "praise de Lawd!"

There were handsome young girls, some so light-skinned that they seemed out of place among the dark-skinned throng, but their voices had the same soft burr as they waved to the regiments marching by and called them "de Lawd's deliverin' army."

Some of them rode in carts, others on muleback. Some pushed each other in wheelbarrows. Others plodded along on foot. Many had come from far distances and were close to starvation and collapse when they found the army.

An old man with a mop of woolly white hair attached himself to Cord. "Li'l Massa, Ole Uncle gwine carry yo' drum. Ole Uncle carry whateber Li'l Massa wants he carry. Ole Uncle gwine whereber Li'l Massa gwine."

For two days he trudged beside Cord, babbling away in his purry voice. He carried whatever baggage Cord was glad to be rid of, including the spoils of his foraging with Bill Foster. But after two days he could not keep the pace and dropped behind.

"Ole Uncle wait fo' Li'l Massa," the weary voice said, following Cord down the road and losing itself in the sound of marching feet as they stirred up clouds of dust.

Cord set his lips tight and marched with his eyes forward.

Another day, a large black woman who had once been a plantation slave embraced Cord.

"We'uns done heered dis wuz an army ob debils fum hell, but praise de Lawd, praise de Lawd," she sobbed, "it's de Lawd's own babes an' sucklin's!"

Cord extracted himself with all the dignity of his affronted fifteen years while his fellow soldiers roared with laughter. The big woman stood on the roadside as the column marched on. She swayed and moaned, and even above the sound of trampling feet could be heard her "Praise de Lawd!"

" 'Tain't right," argued Ira Miles, " 'tain't right to have them thinking we're here just to free the slaves. We're fighting secession. This slavery business has just been hung onto us."

"Sure, but we might as well kill two birds with one stone," was Jennie's lighthearted opinion.

The men knew that Uncle Billy often talked to the runaway slaves. He was kind, patriarchal, but stern as he urged them to return to their masters until a later day, because the army could only feed itself and must move faster than they were able. Freedom did not mean the chance to stop working, he told them, but the chance to begin working for themselves when the right time came; and he asked them not to harm their masters. He not only talked to the hordes of fugitive slaves himself, but he sent their own preachers back through the country with instructions to spread the gospel of work and patient waiting.

Some 25,000 slaves, freed by the Emancipation Proclamation but largely helpless, joined the marching columns, but General Sherman's words turned all but seven thousand away. These were the able-bodied men who could work with the advance guard as it cleared roads, built bridges and wrecked railroads. They followed through to the end, earning their way as part of the army.

Some of the Federals were already in Milledgeville when the Fourteenth Corps marched in on November 24th. A brief rest period was called, during which men visited the capitol building and came away flaunting five-hundred-dollar Confederate bank notes, great packets of which had been left behind when the legislators fled in haste two days before. The Yankees used them to light their pipes and kindle their fires.

When the drums sounded, the Fourteenth Corps moved on briskly to Sandersville. Enemy troops were known to be ahead, but closing in on them they captured the troops without having to fire a shot. The triumphal march continued, and men sang as they marched. They cheered Uncle Billy when he galloped his horse in the fields beside them. They laid bets with each other as to whether the war was won, or not.

Another day of progress and the temper of the men became less jaunty, and far more stern. Shadowlike men, wearing tatters of Federal blue, crept into camp at night. They were gaunt and emaciated, with hunted eyes, and they wept at the sight of food and the flag. They told of he horrors they had been through in Andersonville Prison, where Union prisoners starved in the midst of plenty. The men of the Tenth were shocked into fury at the ghastly look of the escaped prisoners and their tales of suffering endured. Eagerly they asked for news of Lieutenant Colonel Dickerson and the men from their ranks who had been taken prisoner after the battle of Buzzard's Roost. But they met no one who knew of them.

"They's thousands of us fellows still there," said a soldier who looked more dead than alive.

"Ten thousand men or more have died there," another said, "and there'll be many more unless you get there soon."

"Uncle Billy will do something," Cord said, stirred by the dreadful tales.

"He can't do everything," Ira added, "but we're in it to help him all we can."

At the same time, newspapers picked up in the towns they were marching through added to the indignation they were feeling. These were filled with fiery denunciations of the "infamous spawn of perdition" which made up the "invading hosts." They cried frantic enjoinders to the citizens of Georgia to rise against them in defense of their native soil. "Obstruct and destroy all the roads in Sherman's front, flank, and rear, and his army will soon starve in your midst," one editor exhorted. The men, who had foraged and were feasting as a result, laughed as they ate turkey and beefsteak, and spread honey on their corn bread.

They knew what their own orders were: that property should be unmolested where there was no civilian resistance to the advance of the army. But, "should the inhabitants burn bridges, obstruct roads, or otherwise manifest local hostility, the army commanders shall order and enforce devastation more or less relentless, according to the measure of such hostility. The commander of the troops on the spot will deal harshly with the inhabitants nearby, to show them that it is not in their interest to impede our movements."

When slashed roads and desultory fighting halted the progress of the Fourteenth Corps, they knew they acted under orders when they burned mills and cotton gins. Houses were burned more frequently, and barns. The soldiers had a way of saying that some things happened "by accident." Few officers doubted but that it was by intention, but there was little they could do about it. Many of the soldiers, drunk with conquest, were becoming unruly.

Day after day Cord saw, almost as if it were for the first time, the grief and terror of utterly helpless women and children, and it made him feel sick at heart.

"But this is war," said Ira, who had recently returned from a foraging party, "and the Johnnies started it."

"I just hope we Yanks will give it to 'em so hot an' heavy that there'll never be another war," Jennie added.

"It wouldn't be so bad," Ira declared, "if they weren't so consarned scared of us from all this newspaper yelling about the 'vile dregs of northern cesspools, hell-hounds, ravishers, incendiaries,' and all the rest of the pretty names they call us. They just won't believe it when we don't play the part, and they sometimes simply drive the fellows to do things they never would have thought of doing."

Jennie stirred the coals. Over them a young pig was roasting which he and Cord had got that afternoon on an unofficial foraging expedition of their own.

"Gosh, Irie," Jennie began with a grin, "Cord here looked like a vile dreg all right when he come out of a chicken coop this afternoon with a turkey in one fist and a rooster in t'other. He'd wrung the necks of 'em both when an old lady come out of a house we thought was empty. She started bawlin' somethin' about the turkey she'd been fattenin' for somebody's birthday."

"What'd Cordie do?"

"Aw shucks." Cord felt himself blushing, but he knew he'd rather tell it than listen to Jennie. "I gave it to her, of course, an' took a pig instead."

"Sure he gave it to her, the tenderhearted laddie, mostly picked an' cleaned, too. She was that pleased she gave him the pig."

"One o' de Lawd's own sucklin's," teased Ira. "Never mind, Cordie, roast young pig's as good as turkey, any day. But say," he was suddenly serious, "I'm a vile dreg of a drum major for not reporting these private foraging parties of yours. You'll sure get into trouble one of these days if you don't lay off."

He had a good deal more to say about it later that night, and his warning was sufficient to keep the boys in line for more than a week.

The Tenth was on rear-guard duty near Louisville, Georgia, when Cord met Tommy Branch, whose father was near with the divisional wagons. Tommy carried a gun now, almost as big as he was.

"Bridge over Rocky Comfort Creek has been burned," Tommy announced. "The army can't advance until the pontoniers build another. If we have to set here a while we might as well go adventuring."

Cord let out a whoop of joy. That was just what he had been waiting for for a long time. He called to Jennie, and the three boys set out.

A little distance down the road along the creek, they came to an avenue of trees that led up to a handsome, white-columned plantation house. It looked empty. The grounds around the house were littered with refuse, and the lawn was cut by wagon tracks and hoofmarks. The boys decided that it would be a good place to look around, when two ladies came out the front door. They were shawled and bonneted, and both were greatly agitated. One of them was crying. The other addressed the boys in a severe voice.

"Have you come to rob us, too?"

Cord and Jennie were all for turning back without answering, but Tommy said smartly, "We want some chickens."

"Look at them, sister," shrilled the one who had been crying, "mere children, robbing and destroying!"

The other tried to quiet her.

"We're not robbers, ma'am," Jennie defended. "We're foragers. The army must eat."

"Foragers, but not robbers!" was the scoffing retort. "Do you hear him, sister?"

"Young man," she said to him after a moment, "can you tell me where to find your general? We've been robbed of our jewels. My sister's diamonds were rudely snatched from her. It's terrible. Surely your officers will not permit such an outrage."

"No, ma'am, they won't," Cord assured her. He stepped up to them briskly, eager to do what he could, feeling that somehow it would make amends, even if only to himself, for the cruel horseplay he had indulged in with Bill Foster.

"Aw, come on an' forage," Tommy said disgustedly.

Jennie had stepped forward to stand beside Cord. The two older boys then offered to escort the ladies to the encampment where an officer could be found.

"They were horrible Turkish-looking creatures," one of the sisters said as she described the robbers.

"Zouave regiment," Cord explained, "probably Seventeenth New York."

"They wear fancy uniforms," Jennie added, "tight blouse fastened down, huge baggy trousers gathered at the ankle, and a bright red sash wound around their waists."

"And if you want to know how they get into their sashes," Cord added, "they do it by fastening one end to a tree and turning themselves round an' round until they get to the tree."

The ladies were far more interested in telling the boys how they had been robbed by the men who wore the sashes.

Cord knew the Seventeenth was a lawless lot. He said what he had heard an officer say once of them: "Just a bunch of Bowery bums. They've all done time."

The ladies, walking slowly in their high-heeled slippers, shivered and drew their shawls more closely around their shoulders.

Tommy trudged behind them dragging his gun. He had nothing to say.

The sound of riders approaching could be heard and soon a foraging party trotted up to them from around a bend in the road. The boys stepped aside to let them pass. The ladies shrank back in terror. Cord saw an officer whom he knew and promptly hailed him.

"Captain Smith, sir, here's some ladies that's been robbed."

The captain wheeled his horse and pulled up beside them. "Hello, Foote, what does this mean?"

The sisters answered for Cord with a more lurid story than the one they had told the boys.

The captain interrupted them and turned to Cord. "What do you know about this, Foote?"

"Nothing, sir, but I think they were Zouaves."

"Three horrible Turkish-looking creatures," one of the sisters said and the other began to cry again.

"Can't we take a look around for them, sir?" asked Tommy, fondling his gun.

The captain advised the ladies to go back to their house while he and his men made a search for the robbers. He fired a few shots to attract other foraging parties, and the sound sent the ladies scurrying over the road despite their high heels. Two other parties soon came up, and all joined in the hunt through surrounding woods and swamps for the horrible Turkish-looking creatures.

During the afternoon, the foragers began straggling back to the plantation with nothing to show for their efforts. Then Tommy, more from curiosity than anything else, thought he'd have a look into the deserted slave cabins as they sauntered by them. He was poking about the door of one of them with his gun when three men shouldered past him, throwing him down. They started on a run toward the swamp, but Tommy scrambled up and fired his gun to attract Captain Smith and his men. Cord and Jennie yelled their loudest, and the chase was on.

Fifty men shortly closed in on the fugitive three, who were marched back to the house. Captain Smith ordered them to deliver the diamonds immediately. The men did. They were badly frightened, since their own officers had threatened to shoot at sight any of the command who were caught in unsoldierly acts. Explanation of their presence was demanded.

One of them, acting as spokesman, said that they had dropped out of their own foraging party to hide in the cabin. A second group of foragers had then made off with their horses. Other groups had appeared in such rapid succession that they could only cower in hiding and wait for the way to be clear.

Captain Smith delivered sentence of punishment. "For twenty days you will march at the rear of your regiment, under guard. Each one of you will carry a heavy bag of sand in addition to his accouterments. Each one of you will wear a placard labeling him *Robber*."

The ladies looked highly pleased as they returned to their house with the jewels.

"But we're still dregs," said Jennie to Cord as they made their way back to camp.

Tommy wondered what they were laughing about.

It was nine o'clock before the boys came up with their regiment, for the bridge had been completed in the early afternoon and the columns had advanced through Louisville and beyond. Ira Miles was solemn as Cord and Jennie stood before him.

"You two bummers are in for it this time," he told them. "General Davis wanted a divisional drum corps when we marched through Louisville, and General Morgan sent for us. He was mad as hops when two were missing, and General Davis made the air blue. You'll be danglin' by the thumbs this time tomorrow, or I miss my guess."

The summons came on the march next day for Cord and Jennie to appear before General Morgan in camp that night. The boys had a long time during which to anticipate their punishment. When the hour came to make their appearance, they were nearly sick with apprehension. To make matters worse, the general kept them waiting a long time before he would see them. They could hear him laughing, which made them feel a little easier. When an officer emerged from the tent, Cord recognized Captain Smith.

The boys entered at the heels of an orderly. They could see in the candlelight that General Morgan was smiling.

"What do you young scapegraces mean by being absent without leave?" he barked at them, belying his smile. "Out bushwhacking diamond thieves when you should be drumming for the army. It's disgraceful! I guess the only way I can be sure of a drum corps when I want it is to tie a rope around your necks and the other end around the pommel of my saddle. You're dismissed on good behavior. Hear me? On good behavior!"

Ira Miles roused up with surprise when they returned to

the drummers' tent. The boys were grinning from ear to ear.

"You're too lucky to live," was Ira's disgusted comment when the boys finished telling their story.

Cord would not have minded any punishment that General Morgan might have meted out to him. He had settled a score with himself and that was all that mattered.

The way grew more difficult as they neared Savannah, now known to be the goal of their great march through Georgia. Foragers were constantly harried by enemy cavalry, and foraging became less and less fruitful. There were slashed roads to be cleared every day. As they neared the coast, an increasing number of wide, sluggish creeks slowed their advance. Swampy waters, swirling between high banks, often concealed quicksands. The pontoniers were kept busy building bridges that would safely hold the long train of men and wagons. Often the men had to wait for hours until a bridge was finished so they could move at last.

Pine swamps and wet weather finally put an end to foraging. The men began to talk about oysters and sea food, which most of them had never tasted. But, until they reached the sea, they had to rely on the bacon and hardtack brought from Atlanta in the wagons and now sparingly rationed. This was supplemented by rice, great stacks of which they began to find along the way. The year's harvest had been gathered for threshing and the men helped themselves to it. Hungry soldiers invented their own method of threshing by pounding the hulls from the rice in hollowed-out tree trunks. After two or three hours of pounding, the contents were emptied into a basket for the wind to blow the chaff away. Then they cooked the rice in the dark-colored water that was all they had. It never lost its cypress taste no matter how long it was boiled.

On December 9th, about fourteen miles from Savannah, they came upon the first enemy battery. It was located at the head of a long, straight, narrow causeway that led through a forest of giant pines, and it held them utterly at bay. As the Michigan Tenth dropped back amid the confusion of shelling to give place to the Illinois Second Artillery in command of Lieutenant Stedman, they saw the lieutenant cut in two by an enemy cannon ball. The sickening sight sent them back to the cotton field where they had earlier camped. They were heavy with dread of what might lie before them in this strange, dark country of impassable swamps and towering trees that dripped with crepelike strands of moss.

When the enemy battery evacuated in the night, they were able to advance again—directly, for a time, and then laterally, as they found the road ahead flooded by sluices from the canal. Savannah seemed impregnable within its circle of pine swamps that formed a natural barrier, vastly stronger than man-made moats or bastions. The Tenth settled into camp in a spongy clearing, sharing their trenches with the Seventeenth New York Zouaves. It looked as if the siege of Savannah might be a long and tedious business, so they built gun emplacements by day and learned new gambling games from the Zouaves at night. Cord even began to have some respect for the men who he had once thought could only be admired for the red sashes they wore.

"We may be stuck here all winter," Ira Miles said, "and a cold, wet, wearisome winter on starvation rations it will be for us all."

Cord couldn't agree to the last. The weather was beyond control, but as long as he had his slingshot in his pocket he knew he could furnish some food.

"If I get the rabbit, you can cook the stew."

Ira grinned. "I'll do that, Cordie. An' whyn't you get a nice fat southern crow while you're about it?"

They made the best of their quarters and settled in for the

winter, but no one regretted the news that burst over the camp on the fourteenth of December. Uncle Billy and the Fifteenth Corps had taken Fort McAllister, near the mouth of the Ogeechee River which was their nearest approach to the sea. They had made a quick march down the river, rebuilt a thousand-foot bridge on which to cross, and circled about, approaching the fort from the rear. By a bold charge they had completely possessed it within an hour, capturing seventeen guns and three hundred men. At the same time, a steamer appeared moving slowly up the river with word from the Union fleet that was awaiting news at sea.

In two more days there was open communication with the sea and visible proof in the form of a huge mail from the North. It was welcomed with whoops of joy, for it was the first word the men had had from home in nearly six weeks. Fresh rations were delivered. New clothing was issued. The next few days were lived in a sense of triumph and relief—one mood confusing the other but both heartening.

A week later word came that the enemy had evacuated Savannah. The next day the brigade moved eagerly toward the city on the main road, but they soon found it to be impassable until the canal waters could be drained away. By following the railroad tracks through flooded parts, they arrived at a camping place on higher ground in a strip of pines within two miles of the city. Here they were ordered to build themselves cabins. They fell to with a will, cutting down pines and chinking them with the trailing moss. When it came to furnishings, they used some of the feathery stuff to make comfortable beds.

General Sherman had sent a telegram to President Lincoln and in it he had said, "I beg to present you as a Christmas gift, the city of Savannah, with one hundred and fifty heavy guns and plenty of ammunition, also about twenty-five thousand bales of cotton."

Men repeated it around their cabin fires as they celebrated with a mess of hulled rice and their new rations. The day after Christmas orders came to prepare for a grand review by General Sherman in Savannah. They spent the day cleaning their equipment, polishing brass buttons and the silver mountings of their drums. Gun barrels and scabbards were scoured. The Zouaves even washed their red sashes so the color would be more dazzling.

December 27th was clear and sunny. Cord marched at the head of his company, one pace behind the color-bearer. With bands playing and drums rolling, the blue ranks marched down the wide, oak-lined streets. Deep-eaved mansions stood behind high iron fences. Buildings, mellowed by time, looked empty and withdrawn. Trees with spreading branches trailing moss gave a quiet dignity to the city. There was a quality to Savannah that the armies recruited from western plains and midwestern towns had never seen before.

Every man who marched was conscious of his own shining smartness; conscious of the fact that just as he was a part of the review, he had been a part of all that had led up to it—the long marches, the terrible battles, the cold and the heat, the bitter wind and the drenching rain. Many of them thought of those who were not with them at this, the moment of sure triumph, but it seemed that they were marching, too—

> Tramp, tramp, tramp, the boys are marching,
> Cheer up, comrades, they will come,
> And beneath the starry flag
> We shall breathe the air again
> Of the free land in our own beloved home.

At last they came to Uncle Billy. They had never seen him as he was now, in the full-dress uniform of a major general, with stars and gold braid and tassels, and flashing accouterments. Even his handsome horse was in full cavalry regalia.

"Uncle Billy's dolled up like a duke," Jennie whispered to Cord.

No one so much as turned his head; no one missed a step; not a drumbeat was blurred; but the men couldn't suppress their smiles of pride as they marched past their commanding general. Many had seen him in a slouch hat and ulster by a river at an early morning crossing; some had seen him prowling about a campfire in red flannel drawers and a worn dressing gown; Cord had seen him naked, swimming in the river like any of his soldiers. That was Uncle Billy—a great man, a brilliant general, but still one of them.

When tattoo sounded through the beautiful old city at sundown, the tramp of marching feet had died away in the distance. Back in camp that night there were oysters to eat—fried oysters, roast oysters, oysters on the half shell. Michigan had arrived at the sea.

CHAPTER XIII

THE END OF THE WAR was in sight, but the end of Cord's three-year enlistment was at hand. Cord longed with all that was in him to stay with the army until the war was won. He tried every possible way to get permission to stay on, but because of his age and his size he was denied re-enlistment.

"Couldn't I just stay on without permission?"

From Lieutenant Tom down to Ira Miles the answer was the same: "That's something no one can do."

The Tenth was quartered in an old brick building in Savannah, from which they went daily to the wharves to help unload boats. Cord applied to the captain of a freighter for a berth. The captain took one look at him, shook his head and said, "You're not big enough."

Raw, wet January days moved on. Cord celebrated his sixteenth birthday with the men of the regiment trying to make up to him for the disappointment he was feeling. He might be three years older than when he had first marched away from Flint, but he was little taller. He was still thin and pale, with a thick shock of brown hair and big blue eyes that had a way of saying more than his tongue.

"Maybe you'll grow some if you go home and feed up good for a few months," Ira Miles suggested.

"Aw shucks, Footey," said one of the men who had not re-enlisted for veteran service, "whyn't you go when the goin's good? I'm countin' the days to February sixth."

Orders for the advance into South Carolina had been given. Cord would march with his regiment as far as Sisters' Ferry. There, the thirty who were leaving would board ship for the north. Most of the men could hardly wait.

When the Tenth set forth on the Louisville road a few days later, as rear guard for the brigade on its way to South Carolina, Cord had a chance to talk with Captain Dunphy. They were waiting in a muddy field for the wagon train to be corduroyed through a swamp. The logs used were green and the bark peeled off before a half dozen wagons were over; then the water froze on the slippery logs. Even with all hands helping, the passage of the wagons became a desperate journey.

Cord told the captain that he wanted to stay on with the men who were going to see the war through to its end.

Captain Dunphy smiled at him kindly. "See that stretch of muck just ahead there, Foote?" he asked by way of reply. "We'll be wading through miles of that during the next few weeks, and a lot of it is so deep that it'd be over your head."

Too small, Cord thought bitterly.

He drummed as he had never drummed before, though his fingers were cold and his heart leaden. The men marched and the wagons moved through the swampy coastal land of Georgia into South Carolina. The going was as difficult as any they had ever had, but the drummers carried them through it.

Uncle Billy was waiting ahead at Sisters' Ferry, and Cord thought desperately that he would present his plea himself to his commanding general; but when they reached their campground by the river Uncle Billy was not there. Clerks were already at work on the mustering-out rolls as the regiment prepared for a stiff campaign.

At noon of February 6th, the thirty non-veterans were summoned to headquarters and given their dismissal rolls. They were informed that a steamer would be waiting to take them to Savannah at six in the morning. Cord set his lips. He had his orders, the last he would receive from the army.

Walking back to the drummers' tent with some of his friends, he stopped with them to watch a group of horsemen ride by. The horsemen were led by a small man with important-looking red whiskers.

"That's Little Kil," someone said.

"General Kilpatrick!" Cord gasped. He had heard of the fiery little commander of cavalry who had done so much to make General Sherman's campaign a success. Cord watched him closely. General Kilpatrick must have been small to start with. He must have heard the same thing said to him that Cord heard so often; but it hadn't stopped him.

"Kil-Irishman's more like it," said Ira. "I've heard he's the hardest hell-driver of an Irishman there is in the army."

Bill Foster, who was known to be disdainful of all officers except General Sherman, exclaimed, "Well, if I was one of his hossback riders I'd take his trailin' mustachios an' tie 'em around his ears."

Cord laughed at the picture.

"Footey's feelin' happy," teased Bill. "He's leavin' us tomorrow."

Eddie Knowlton came up from behind and joined them as they strolled back to their quarters. "Footey leavin' us tomorrow?" Eddie asked, unbelieving.

Everyone in the regiment knew how hard the drummer boy of Company F had tried to stay on. Eddie was only expressing the surprise and regret the regiment felt that Cord had not succeeded.

"Got my papers," Cord said glumly.

Eddie swore roundly.

"Just how I feel," said Cord.

They slumped along in the mud, saying nothing. Then Eddie drew off a silver ring he was wearing and gave it to Cord. "Footey," he said solemnly, "you can't get away from the old Tenth if you try."

Cord gazed at the ring, then he slipped it on a finger. "Thanks, Eddie. I'm going to wear it as long as I live."

Next morning Cord sounded reveille for the last time.

"I heerd you," Bill Foster grumbled as he came out of his tent. "What d'you think you're callin' for—Day o' Judgment?"

Ira was cooking the drummers' breakfast. All through the camp was the stir of preparation for the day's advance.

"Next time I cook another meal it'll be a long way from here, and next time you eat, Cordie, you'll be a long way from here."

"I'm not going home, Irie," Cord announced. "I'm going to stay with the regiment."

Ira kept at his cooking, seeming not to have heard what Cord said. When the bacon was ready to offer to Cord, he said kindly, "It's tough luck, Cordie, but you know you can't do that."

And that was the worst of it: Cord knew that Ira was right. They were both soldiers, and a soldier obeyed orders.

Cord nodded silently and put some bacon into his mouth so he would not have to speak. The rebellion he had felt that morning as he drummed men out of sleep and into the day's advance collapsed before Ira's matter-of-fact acceptance of things as they had to be.

"You've still got your drum, Cordie, you'll always have that, and no one can take away from us what we've been through together."

After breakfast Cord went to the tent for his belongings. He shouldered his blanket roll, haversack, and drum. He was ready to leave. Ira walked down to the river with him. The *H. H. Pierson*, engines athrob, was waiting at the landing. The twenty-nine other men, impatient to get home, were already aboard.

"Here we are," said Ira. "Good luck, Cordie!"

"Good luck, Irie!"

Cord climbed aboard and Ira hurried back to the brigade.

Amid the noise and clatter as the boat got under way, Cord heard in the distance the rhythmic roll and rat-a-tat-tat of the drums as the new campaign began without him.

The dark waters of the Savannah River at flood swirled around the big boat, as three years ago the waters of the Mississippi had swirled around another boat. One was relentlessly sweeping Cord away from all that he most desired, as the other had swept him into it.

The *H. H. Pierson* wormed her way through a dark jungle of tangled live oaks trailing Spanish moss and standing deep in water. The swift current and circuitous course of the flooded river taxed the skill of the pilot. Frequently, when they turned a bend, gnarled branches tore and clawed at the boat. Near nightfall the boat was caught in the great limbs of a fallen tree, which wrecked the pilothouse and held them up. Cord watched gloomily as the sailors worked to free the boat and repair the pilothouse. He speculated on his chances for escape and return to the regiment, but knew that they amounted to nothing.

The boat docked at Savannah at noon the following day and the thirty men from the Tenth transferred to a small seagoing steamer that carried them without incident to Hilton Head on the coast of South Carolina. It was a warm day and very still. The clear light and salty air put new life into the men after their weeks of milling about in dank oak swamps. There was a Soldiers' Home at Hilton Head, with straw bunks and open fireplaces; but except for the time it took Cord to cook his bacon and coffee, and to consult the army paymaster, he spent the hours on the long pier which reached out into the ocean.

By noon of the next day, when the transport *Orago* hove into Hilton Head, a film had come between sun and sea, and a metallic dullness blurred the horizon. Four hundred soldiers crowded aboard and the two-masted schooner soon set sail for New York.

Cord roamed the top deck to see what he could see and to ask questions of whoever would answer them. The sails, spread to catch the first vagrant breeze, hung limp in the lifeless air.

When a wind finally came, it brought weather with it. At first there was only a kind of slow, quiet lifting of air and ocean, but the sailors knew what was coming and mounted the yards to haul in canvas; then the level sea began to heave in great, slow swells. The swells formed into rollers, sweeping majestically from the horizon which seemed to draw in around them. Then the rollers broke up into surging waves. The ship began to plunge through them, creaking and groaning. The wind shrieked in the empty halyards. The ocean roared.

Cord watched the terrifying transformation from the top deck. Two men from the Tenth were beside him. One was a tailor by trade and he had crossed from Germany not too many years before. The hazards of an ocean voyage were still vivid to him.

"Ach, Little Foote, you vill be zee-sick!" he commiserated. "How about you?"

"Nah, not me. I had it vunst. I'm—vot you say, like—tough?"

Cord's other companion, a Great Lakes sailor, was more helpful. "Feelin' all right, Footey?"

"Well, Jim, I feel like I'm swingin' an' can't stop."

They found a sheltered place on the deck and sat down.

"Now, don't think about the motion of the boat," Jim advised. "Look at something way off. Don't watch the water and you'll be all right."

They stayed there together until after dark when the great waves began to break over the boat and would have wet them through, then they went below. Three tiers of bunks lined the six-feet-high room. A lantern swayed in the darkness and by the dim light Cord found an empty bunk and climbed in. He lay with his head to the bow, and for the next few hours seemed at one moment to stand on his head and the next moment to stand on his feet as the ship plunged and rocked. The noise of the straining ship was deafening, the atmosphere was fetid with close-packed bodies, and sick men groaned in their misery. Now and again someone opened a porthole for a breath of air, but when water poured in, it was quickly closed.

Once the big boat stood still and quivered for a moment as if it had struck a rock. Men rolled out of their bunks, ready to make a dash for safety. Then the *Orago* plunged on and the men climbed back into their bunks. The passage was worse off Cape Hatteras; from then on the seas began to subside. By midafternoon of the next day the storm had lulled. Cord found the tailor on the upper deck, looking white and miserable.

"What's the matter, Sammy?" he teased. "Gosh, you're so white I can see right through you. I guess you ain't so tough as you think."

There was a square hole in the top deck with a rail around it; below was the cook's galley. Here, a few men who cared to eat anything let down their mess tins to be filled. Cord's came back to him with three small, round sea biscuits and a chunk of pork three inches square. His tin cup was filled with bitter-tasting coffee that had been made with condensed sea water. After a swallow or two that nearly choked him, he emptied it out, threw away the cold and greasy pork when he couldn't get his teeth into it, and made a meal of the damp sea biscuits.

The *Orago*, her sails furled, steamed into New York harbor in the late afternoon, sixty hours after she had left Hilton Head. Her passengers disembarked at the Battery. With Jim and Sammy, Cord found a room nearby, then the three set out to see the city. The first thing Cord saw was a large custard pie at a homemade cookery counter. It was cut in four quarters which he ate in such ravenous succession that the woman behind the counter could only gasp her amazement.

"Mercy on us, boy, ain't you never had no pie before?"

"Not lately."

The most impressive thing about New York was the variety and quantity of good things to eat. They stopped frequently just to fill themselves up with some kind of food. Cord felt as if he never would be full.

After the pie, the next to catch Cord's eye was a banner of lights heading a brass band on Broadway, which led them straight to P. T. Barnum's Circus. They saw everything from trapeze artists to lions and tigers, the fat lady and the living skeleton. Over and over again they asked each other if this was the same world where, only a few hundred miles south, men were starving and fighting and dying. They found the army paymaster in an office on Bleeker Street. Only when Cord received the considerable balance of his back pay and his transportation home, did he really feel that he was out of the army.

On the 15th of February Cord arrived in Flint by stage from Fentonville. He stood still for a moment, holding his drum tight to him, then he turned up Saginaw Street toward home.

"Ma?" he called, then "Pa?" as he walked in the front door of the house.

After a while he began to wonder if it would not be easier to be surrounded by Rebs than to be welcomed back by family, friends and neighbors. Everyone wanted to hear about his adventures, and no one seemed to mind how often he told the same stories. When he went out to the barn, the banties didn't know who he was and ran squawking away from him until he eased them back with a handful of corn. The heifer had long since grown to be a cow. The guinea pig cage was empty.

He returned to the house and went up to his old room. There were the birds' eggs which he had sent home from time to time, carefully laid in boxes. And there were the birds which his mother had had stuffed for him. Michigan would never see their like on the wing, of that he was certain. He was proud of his collection. Running his hand over the feathers of a mockingbird, he wondered if he would ever see its flight or hear its song again. Suddenly he felt overcome with loneliness for his regiment, for the men who had sworn at him when he drummed reveille and cheered him when he sounded taps. They had lived in such close comradeship for so long, he wondered how he could ever live without them.

"Coridon—dinner's ready!" his mother called up the stairs.

There was no answer. Cord had gone to find old Lacey; only with him could he feel at home.

Day after day the two members of the Drum Corps followed the progress of the Carolina campaign. They searched the papers for every item of news about General Sherman and his army. Their hearts were with the Michigan Tenth, but their fingers had to be content to trace the Tenth's course from point to point—through Columbia to Fayetteville, then on to Goldsboro. The papers told only a fraction of what they wanted to know, and as the spring advanced, Cord felt more and more restless.

He told Pop that he would do anything to get back into the army. And Pop understood why he felt that way, though everyone else told Cord that he ought to be glad to be home.

One April day, when Cord was at the railway station near his sister Hannah's in Whigville, a passenger train came in. At a window in the rear car Cord spied Jim, the former Great Lakes sailor, in uniform. Cord leaped on the steps of the car before the train had stopped and pelted down the aisle to where Jim sat.

"Hi, Jim, where you goin' in that uniform?"

"Crack me up if it ain't Little Foote! I'm goin' to Washington, Footey. Joined up last week with the Veterans' Reserve Corps. Comin' along?"

In the few moments before the train moved on, Cord found out all he could and Jim promised to co-operate.

"See you in Washington!" Cord beamed up at him as the train puffed away.

"Sure, we'll get you in!" Jim promised, waving his pipe as he stood grinning on the back platform.

The next day the news of General Lee's surrender at Appomattox swept the country. Even after four years of heartbreaking struggle, the end seemed to come with a suddenness that made people almost fear to believe that it was the end. Confirmation was unmistakable, but that night there was no desire to celebrate as early victories had been celebrated with bonfires, torchlight parades and exultant oratory. Deep and solemn gratitude filled men's hearts that the Union was safe. Before them was the realization of what lay ahead in the dual task of reconciliation and reconstruction.

One day after another went by. Spring smiled tentatively on the world. People began to give themselves to cautious rejoicing as they became more accustomed to the fact of peace. Cord went again to Whigville to see his sister Hannah and help her with some of the spring chores. Her house was near the railway station and glancing up from his work now and then he saw trains pass through whose locomotives were draped in black. When he started to walk back to Flint, he went to the station to ask the reason; but there was no one there.

It was a gray day and Cord was filled with foreboding as he trudged the rutted country road. When he had gone halfway he began to hear the church bells tolling in Flint, and he hastened his steps to learn what dreadful thing had happened. The streets were strangely deserted as he came into town. The flag at the Court House hung at half-mast. He stopped at the Carleton House for news.

"Why, Cordie, don't you know—haven't you heard—" Sid Rosevelt's face was solemn, his tone hushed. "President Lincoln has been murdered."

Cord turned and walked back into the empty street. Only once before had he felt the way he felt now—when they brought George Jay in from the apple orchard and laid him on his cot, his body still warm, but lifeless.

During the numbing days that followed, Cord realized that thousands of other people felt as he did. It was a personal sense of loss and grief. The nation moved forward under a dark shadow. Gradually personal loss merged with a sense of personal responsibility.

"We've all got just that much more to do," Old Lacey said, "because he isn't with us any more. Even the least of us."

"Even me." Cord was stating a fact he had come to accept. Now it did not seem to matter that he was small.

On Sunday afternoon there was a memorial meeting in front of the Court House. A rapt crowd of men and women pressed about the steps where the speaker stood, and overflowed into the quiet, tree-lined street where the first green of spring was showing. With solemn eloquence of prayer and eulogy, reverent citizens mourned their martyred President. The meeting closed with a reading of Lincoln's own words from his last inaugural address:

"'With malice toward none, with charity for all, with firmness in the right as God gives us to see the right, let us finish the work we are in, to bind up the nation's wounds, to care for him who shall have borne the battle, and for his widows and orphans, to do all which may achieve and cherish a just and lasting peace among ourselves and with all nations.'"

The next day Cord offered himself as an apprentice at the local tin shop. He would do what he could where he could. If he worked hard and learned the business he might, as his father said, someday be able to buy the tin shop and be his own master.

A month later, Flint heard that the home-coming Tenth had received special mention in a grand review in Washington before Generals Grant and Sherman, and President Johnson. The whole state was impatient to welcome its men home, but it was not until late July that the Tenth reached Jackson, eighty miles south of Flint. That was nearer home than the regiment had been in nearly four years. The summer sunshine seemed to have a special brightness and there was hardly a home that was not preparing to welcome some member back. Cord asked for time off from the tin shop and went over to see what Old Lacey was going to do by way of welcome. He found him reading the paper and smoking his pipe as he sat on the shady back stoop.

"Hi, Pop!" Cord saluted. "Michigan forever! Glory or a wooden leg. Say, Pop, let's go down to Jackson, will you?"

The old man looked up over his spectacles, rather vaguely for a moment before the idea caught him. "Well, well, Cordie, what a notion. What a notion."

Cord knew by the light in his eyes that the notion had appealed. "How long d'you suppose they'll be there?"

"Well, the paper here says they're waitin' for pay," Old Lacey answered, "and none too sweet about it, for which you can't blame them. But the pay is likely to come any minute and then they'll skedaddle, so what would we have for our eighty-mile tramp?"

Cord went home dejectedly, only to read in the paper the following day that the soldiers' pay could not possibly arrive for three days more. The townsfolk of Jackson feared rioting, so aroused were the soldiers by the delay. Cord knew what he wanted to do, and he never doubted but that he could get Old Lacey to join him.

Before dawn the next morning he put on his uniform and went over to Old Lacey's, carrying his drum, haversack and blanket roll. He walked around to the side of the house and drummed reveille under the bedroom window. When there was no response, he drummed again, winding up with a noisy flourish and the rippety-roar of the daddy-mammy.

Old Lacey stuck his head out of an upper window. "What in tarnation—" he began.

"C'm'on, Pop, come on, we gotta get goin'!" Cord called to him.

The old man was not to be swept along in such fashion.

After what seemed to Cord an unreasonably long time, he came out dressed but not in uniform.

"Oh, Pop, hustle a bit. Let's get going along."

"Pack o' nonsense," he spluttered. "Pack o' nonsense."

"You're just afraid folks'll think you an old fool," Cord said. "Well, I'm a young one." He drew his hand up in salute. "I'll tell the boys 'hello.' Glory or a wooden leg, I'm off for Jackson." He turned away.

"What, you don't mean you're goin' alone, Cordie?"

"Just try to stop me," answered Cord, without turning, then he began to beat his drum in marching step.

Cord marched past the first house, then the second, drumming lightly so he would not waken too many people. He was almost at the corner when Old Lacey's shout reached him.

"Wait a minute, Cordie. I'll tell Maria I'm goin' too."

The minute was a short one. When Pop appeared in uniform and drumming snappily, Cord knew that he must have been ready to go all along.

Putting away their drumsticks, they marched out of town as quickly and quietly as they could. Pop patted his pocket. "Brought the fife along too, Cordie, there's times when it makes a mighty sweet sound."

In a little while they were marching to their drums again through the green countryside that bordered the windings of the Miller Road. Save for a brief rest at noon, they kept a steady pace until near sundown, when they decided to camp beside a creek just beyond the village of Durand. While Old Lacey set up a small tent shelter, Cord built a fire and fried the bacon.

"Gosh, I've missed this," Cord sighed as they sat against a log eating bacon and buns.

"Right you are," Old Lacey agreed. "It gets into your blood. When you're as old as I am, Cordie, and you think back, you'll know you were never so content as when you were marching with a lot of good fellows on a stiff campaign, even though you were hot or cold and hungry, and afraid you might get shot to pieces the next day. There's somethin' about it, pure contrariness of the critter, maybe—"

"Well, it's not the shooting and killing we're crazy about, I could swear to that."

"No, it's not the shooting and killing. It's the pulling together, Cordie, all on tiptoe to do somethin' big. Some fine day, before you're dead and gone, maybe, Cordie, men will hatch up a way to march together an' do big things without the shooting and killing to spoil it."

The moon came up and the early crickets chorused, but they talked on, scheming out a kind of grand army of reconstruction, the best of war with the bad left out.

"Better bunk down now, Cordie," Pop said. "We've still got a long march before us."

They rolled up in their blankets and sleep came soon.

Another day's marching brought them near Lansing. It rained that night but a good-natured farmer let them spread their blankets on his porch. On the cool, cloudy day that followed, they tried a short cut to which the farmer directed them, but missed the road to Jackson and dusk found them in the Irish Hills. They camped near the Walker Tavern. After supper by their own fire, they went to the tavern for news. A miscellaneous group had gathered on the wide veranda.

"So, you're from the Michigan Tenth," observed a large, important-looking man who heard Old Lacey's query. "You, too, my boy?" he asked Cord, who found himself wondering what was so familiar about him as he talked on in a fine, booming voice. "Pretty rough lot, those fellows, pretty rough lot. Been rioting for their pay. It's shameful." He was looking at a Jackson paper.

They listened while a voluble citizen of Jackson told how the soldiers had gone to the paymaster's house in noisy resentment, surrounding the place, yelling, shouting, and throwing stones. "They'd oughta know the man couldn't give 'em nothin' till he had it to give."

"A pretty rough lot," came the big voice again, and again Cord wondered where he had heard it before.

"A pretty rough lot, eh?" Old Lacey mocked as he confronted the speaker. "Well, sir, just what kind of gentle sisters do you think it took to charge the heights of Missionary Ridge and batter down Atlanta, and push through the forests and swamps of Georgia and Carolina with nothing to eat but what they could gather by the way? Lord a'mighty, man, I recollect a speech of yours—something about the state of Michigan being ready to 'resist to the blood.' It was a grand speech, and it fired some mighty brave young fellows to do just that. Here they are, home again, the ones that lived through it, conquerors! 'A pretty rough lot' you say."

"Stop, my good man, I meant no offense, I assure you."

Then Cord remembered. It was no other than Colonel Fenton, whose words had first fired him to go to war.

He sounded sincerely sorry and soon had Old Lacey on a bench beside him with a conciliatory cigar. Cord settled into a big chair and listened to the talk of politics and reconstruction. Sometimes he even dared to put in a word of his own. Most of the time he dreamed, thinking what a very long time ago it seemed since this big man's eloquence had stirred him. He wondered what life would have been like if he hadn't gone to war.

"Your pardon, sir," Old Lacey said as he got up to go, "but I've seen that rough lot down there do the noble things you sent them out for to do, and of course they want their pay. What's shameful is that it's not there so they can get on home. And one more thing you fine orators better remember—when a lot of high-spirited young fellows once learn how to get things by force, it ain't always so easy for them to forget the habit. Good night, sir. Thank you for a pleasant evening, sir."

He and Cord strolled off together.

"Gosh, Pop, you certainly gave it to him hot an' heavy."

"Did I, Cordie?" Pop grinned. "Well, there ain't nobody can insult the Michigan Tenth while Old Lacey's got breath to defend it."

"Right you are. But say, Pop, he did make a good speech three years ago, and I'm glad I heard it."

"Mebbe so, Cordie, mebbe so, but you'da been a foot taller by now if you'd had enough to eat. You've grown a good three inches since you got home."

"Makin' up for lost time, Pop. I'll get there yet."

It was noon next day when they reached the woods at the edge of Jackson where the Michigan Tenth was encamped. The savory odors of bacon and coffee wafted to them. The familiar sight of men hovering over campfires, with tents in the background, set their hearts jumping. They approached quietly, then readied themselves for the entrance they had planned during their march together.

"All right, Cordie, let 'er go!"

They crashed out a smart salute in unison, and then Old Lacey with shrilling fife and Cord with rattling drum swung into camp to the tune of "Yankee Doodle," eyes forward, looking neither to one side nor the other. The effect was electric. Men dropped what they were doing with varying expressions of surprise. Some looked sulky, some annoyed, until they realized that their oldest and their youngest had come to greet them—the regiment's first drum major and the drummer boy of Company F. The cheering was immense as comrades swarmed about the two, but fifer and drummer still stepped smartly along, eyes front, oblivious to all until Bill Foster and Jennie were suddenly on top of Cord, and Ira Miles had Old Lacey helpless.

That night there was no rioting in Jackson. The spirit of the reunited drum corps seemed to pervade the camp. A full moon showered its radiance over them and a big bonfire drew them together for a last telling of stories, a last singing of songs.

"You really shoulda been with us, Footey, right to the end. They'd no right to send you home."

Next morning the men received their long-awaited pay. They packed their kits, shook hands with each other, and set off on the different roads that led to home.

"Michigan forever!" The regimental slogan was their farewell, as it would be their greeting when they met again.

Old Lacey and Ira Miles, with Cord between them, set off on the road to Flint—Old Lacey to return to his Maria, Cord to go back to the tin shop, and Ira to go on to his farm which was in the Upper Peninsula. They drummed as they started out, tapping the turns with a burl and staccato that lifted their feet and set them on their way as into a new campaign. Other men, following other roads, heard the distant sound and fell into a steadier pace. Once, the drums had filled them with the feeling that they could do big things, meet dangers bravely, cover long marches. The rataplan had rolled up their individual wills into one will that had staying power and final strength for victory. Gradually the sound dimmed in the distance, except for the three members of the Drum Corps who were making it.

Cord looked down at the silver ring on his finger. As long as he lived he would belong to the Michigan Tenth, and the Tenth belonged to something far greater—the Union they had fought to save.

INDEX

INDEX

Alport, Gill, 86
Anderson's Cross Roads, 123, 124, 128, 129, 141
Andersonville Prison, 165, 219
Appomattox, 240
Army of the Cumberland, 58, 65, 85, 93, 102, 107, 121, 148, 191
Army of the Mississippi, 36, 149
Army of the Ohio, 191
Army of the Potomac, 121, 149
Army of the Tennessee, 191
Athens, Alabama, 104
Atlanta, Georgia, 176, 183, 190, 191, 193, 195, 196-98, 209

Barnum's Circus, P. T., 239
Beach, Captain, 24, 46, 155
Bickerdycke, Mother, 181
Blair, Governor, 18
Bootleggers, 66
Bragg, General Braxton, 80
Branch, Sergeant (later Lieutenant) Thomas, 68, 74-75, 90, 91-92, 94-95, 96-100, 126, 133, 231

Branch, Tommy, 68, 74-75, 90, 92, 96, 97, 98, 99, 100, 126-27, 221
Bridgeport, Alabama, 116, 117, 121, 123, 173
Bull Run, 21
Burnett, Major, 111-13, 194
Burnside, General Ambroise E., 153, 154, 156
Buzzard's Roost, Georgia, 164, 173

Cairo, Illinois, 34, 56, 57
Camp Big Springs, 44
Cape Hatteras, 237
Carson, Zeb, 146, 147, 149-150
Centerville, Georgia, 205
Chandler, Senator, 18
Charleston, Tennessee, 152, 153
Chattahoochie River, 189
Chattanooga, Tennessee, 10, 101, 105, 126, 133, 134, 142, 149, 150, 156, 157, 164, 165, 199, 201
Cherry Creek, 63, 67, 85, 92, 101, 171

[251]

Chickamauga, Georgia, 121, 150, 152, 159-60
Chickamauga River, 143, 146, 150
Chris (Cord's dog), 74, 75, 82, 85, 92-93, 103-04
Cleburne, General Patrick R., 193
Columbia, Tennessee, 104, 240
Columbus, Kentucky, 57
Confederate States of America, 17
Contraband camp, 107-09
Corinth, Mississippi, 37, 40, 42
Cowles, Adjutant, 40-41, 42
Cracker line, 87-90, 96-100, 123, 133
Cumberland River, 35, 92

Dallas, Tennessee, 133, 134
Davis, General, 141, 225
Decatur, Georgia, 209
Decherd, 173
DeGraff, drummer, 33, 41, 151
Descriptive Roll, 47, 49
Detroit, Michigan, 21, 31, 167
Detroit and Milwaukee Railroad, 30
Detroit Free Press, 18, 32
Dickerson, Lieut. Colonel, 40, 42, 47, 49, 63-64, 71, 72, 162, 164, 165, 219
Dilger, Captain, 180
Dismissal Roll, 233
Donelson, Fort, 36
Drummer Boy of Shiloh, 12
Drummer boys, 13
Dunphy, Captain, 194, 195, 232
Durand, Michigan, 244

Eleventh Army Corps, 121
Emancipation Proclamation, 218

Farmington, 44
Fayetteville, 240
Fenton, Colonel, 19-20, 22, 246
Fenton Light Guard, 22
Fentonville, Michigan, 167-68, 239
Fifteenth Army Corps, 228
Fish, Dr., 50-51
Fish, George, 51, 52
Fish, Jim, 172
Fisher, Wardie, 67, 68, 75, 92, 128, 157, 160

Flint, Michigan, 7, 17, 168, 239, 241, 248
Flint Historical Museum, 11
Flint Union Grays, 21
Florence, Alabama, 199
Foote, Corydon Edward, 8
Foote, George, 20, 22, 154, 172
Foraging parties, 211, 212-14, 219-20
Foster, Bill, 113-17, 121, 126-27, 128, 135-140, 141, 157, 173, 180, 199, 213-14, 233, 234, 248
Fourteenth Army Corps, 65, 121, 134, 143, 156, 193, 195, 205, 206, 218, 220
Fraternization, 135-40
Furlough, 162, 165-71

Gambling, 66
Gardner, Charlie, 20, 21, 23, 130
Garesche, Colonel, 81
Gettysburg, Pennsylvania, 102
Gladiator, steamship, 34-36
Goldsboro, 240
Gould, Benjamin A., 13
Grand Army of the Republic, 11
Granger, General Gordon, 148
Grant, General Ulysses S., 36, 93, 102, 134, 148, 195, 205, 242
Groves, Dr., 52-54
Guerrillas, 58, 89, 94-96, 202-04
Guild, Captain, 21

Halleck, General Henry W., 93
Hamburg Landing, Tennessee, 36, 37, 47, 48
Hannah (Cord's married sister), 28, 86, 240, 241
Hardee, General William J., 193
Hart, Captain Noah H., 126, 132, 140, 153
Henry, Fort, 36
Hilton Head, South Carolina, 236
Holly, Michigan, 28, 30, 48, 171
Hood, General John Bell, 197, 199
Hooker, General Joseph, 121, 144, 149, 182
Hughes, Fletcher, 117
Huntsville, Alabama, 104, 200

Illinois 2nd Artillery, 227
Illinois 68th Artillery, 68, 77, 79
Illinois 10th Infantry, 163, 165
Illinois 60th Infantry, 38, 39, 102, 133, 140, 164, 179, 184, 190, 192
Illinoistown, Illinois, 34
Indianapolis, Indiana, 167
Indiana 6th Infantry, 148
Indian Wars, 17
Irish Hills, 245

Jackson, Andrew, 17, 19
Jackson, Michigan, 243, 247-48
Jay, George, 24, 31, 33, 35, 36, 37, 38, 39, 40, 48, 60, 65, 68, 70, 102, 106, 108, 109, 135-36, 139, 143, 153, 160, 173, 177, 189, 192-93, 200, 208, 241
Jefferson Barracks, 47, 49-54
Jennings, John, 160, 177, 201, 204, 208, 210, 248
Jeremiah, 107-08
Jonesboro, Georgia, 193
Johnson, Andrew, 242
Johnston, General Joseph E., 175

Kennesaw Mountain, 180, 183-89
Kentucky 21st Infantry, 150
Kieffer, Harry M., 12
Kilpatrick, General Hugh J., 233
Kline, Katherine Foote, 8
Knowlton, Edie, 234
Knoxville, Tennessee, 128, 152, 153, 156

Lacy, Pop (Old Lacey), 18, 19, 22-25, 33, 36, 37, 48, 60, 62, 66, 71, 83-84, 101, 102, 105, 106, 107, 116, 123, 125, 126, 141, 150, 152, 154, 160, 170-71, 200, 240, 243-48
Lansing, Michigan, 245
Lavergne, Tennessee, 89, 90
Lee, General Robert E., 240
Lily Belle, steamboat, 55-57
Lincoln, Abraham, 21, 195, 205, 206, 208, 228, 241-42
Little Tennessee River, 155
Long March, the, 154-58
Longstreet, General James, 156

Lookout Mountain, 117, 144, 145, 173
Lost Mountain, 183
Louisville, Georgia, 221, 225, 232
Louisville, Kentucky, 58, 90, 167
Louisville and Nashville Railway, 58
Love's Ferry, 123
Low, Sergeant, 188
Lum, Colonel, 26, 27, 76

Macon, Georgia, 209
Malachi, 69, 71-72
Mappers, 178
Maps, campaigns of Michigan 10th Infantry 1862-1865, 16, 125
Marietta, Georgia, 187
Maryville, Tennessee, 156, 157
McAllister, Fort, 228
McCook, Colonel, 128
Meade, General George, 102
Michigan 4th Cavalry, 172
Michigan 1st Infantry, 20, 21
Michigan 2nd Infantry, 21
Michigan 3rd Infantry, 21
Michigan 4th Infantry, 204
Michigan 10th Infantry, 8, 22; campaigns of, 1862-1865 (map), 16, 125
Miles, George, 172
Miles, Ira, 24, 33, 44, 45, 48, 65, 66, 88, 116, 117, 150, 153, 156, 160, 177, 189, 191, 192, 195, 208, 209, 210, 214, 225, 227, 231, 234, 248
Milledgeville, Georgia, 209, 218
Missionary Ridge, 141, 143, 144-49, 157, 163
Mississippi River, 34, 49, 55
Morgan, General George W., 141, 161, 164, 225, 226
Morgan's Raiders, 58
Morganton, Tennessee, 155
Murfreesboro, Tennessee, 76, 85, 86, 88, 89, 90, 93, 98, 101, 102, 103, 171

Nashville, Tennessee, 58, 61, 62, 66, 67, 73, 82, 85, 90, 92, 100, 164, 167, 171
Nashville Turnpike, 89

Index

Negroes, 107-09, 200, 215-18
New Albany, Indiana, 58
New York City, 238
New York 17th Zouaves, 222-23, 227, 229
Nicholasville, 58
Nicholls, Lieutenant, 94, 95

Official Records of the Civil War, 10
Ogeechee River, 228
Ohio 1st Infantry, 180
Ohio River, 34, 40
Oostenaula River, 183
Orago, steamship, 236-38
Orchard Knob, 148
Owensville Pike, 59
Owosso, Michigan, 8
Owosso Public Library, 10

Parcelo, Del, 86
Peach Tree Creek, 190
Pierson, H. H., steamship, 235
Pine Mountain, 183
Pittsburgh Landing, 35, 36
Pontoon bridges, 143-44, 150, 157, 178-79, 189, 226
Pope, General Nathaniel, 36

Rebel yell, 91
Recollections of a Drummer Boy, 12
Re-enlistment, 162
Reinhardt, Vic, 12
Resaca, Georgia, 173, 176
Ringgold, Georgia, 151, 163
Rocky Comfort Creek, 221
Rocky Face Ridge, 164-65
Rome, Georgia, 176
Rose, George, 197
Rosecrans, General Franz, 65-66, 80, 81, 93, 96, 100, 102, 105, 134, 199
Rosevelt, Sid, 168, 241
Rough and Ready, 198
Round Forest, 81
Runaway slaves, 107

St. Louis, Missouri, 55
Sallywhite Pike, 72
Sandersville, Georgia, 218

Sanitary Commission, 41, 42, 75, 82
Savannah, Georgia, 10, 226, 227, 228-30, 231, 236
Savannah River, 235
Scaritt, Major, 111
Schofield, Major General John McA., 201-02, 204
Schumacher, Hans, 33, 39
Secession, 17
Sequatchie Valley, 123, 129
Seventeenth Army Corps, 145
Shelbyville, Tennessee, 85, 102, 171
Sheridan, General Philip, 80-81
Sherman, General William T., 142-43, 145, 149, 151, 152, 153, 175, 177-78, 182, 183, 187, 189, 193, 195, 197-98, 205, 206, 207, 208, 210, 212, 217, 218, 228-30, 233, 242
Shiloh, 32-33
Sisters' Ferry, 232, 233
Smith, Captain, 224, 225
Smith's Ferry, Tennessee, 133, 135
Sparling, Dr., 46-47
Stedman, Lieutenant, 227
Stone's River, 59, 61, 75, 76-81, 85, 89, 98, 171
Stevenson, Alabama, 102, 105, 107, 109, 165, 173, 199
Summers, Charlie, 172
Sumter, Fort, 19
Sutlers, 109-13, 197

Tantallon, 173
Tennessee River, 35, 48, 117, 133, 144, 159, 173
Thomas, General George H., 81, 121, 134, 147, 148, 149, 162, 165, 182, 195
Tigris, steamboat, 55-57
Toledo, Ohio, 167
Topographical engineers, 178
Tullahoma, Tennessee, 102, 173
Turner, George, 86
Tyson, Jimmie (Sissie), 68-69, 70, 77, 79-80, 200

Vanderburgh, Lieutenant, 93, 94, 96
Van Dyne, Dr., 50, 51, 52

Index

Veterans' Reserve Corps, 240
Vicksburg, Mississippi, 102

Walden's Ridge, 124
Ward, Andrew, 172
Ward, Charlie, 172
Ward, Mr., 169
Wells, Lew, 132
Wheeler, General Joseph, 124, 128, 135
Whigville, Michigan, 28, 240, 241
White Hall, Georgia, 196, 199

White House Landing, Tennessee, 141, 152, 157
Widow's Creek, 121
Winter quarters, 159-63
Wisconsin 5th Artillery, 133, 135, 140
Wisner, Moses, 18
Wolverine Citizen, The, 21

Yates Sharpshooters, 40-41

Zollicopher House, 59, 167

www.ingramcontent.com/pod-product-compliance
Lightning Source LLC
Chambersburg PA
CBHW072000110526
44592CB00012B/1157